Magnificent
MEALS in a BOWL
COOKBOOK

RECIPE CONVERSIONS

⅛ teaspoon = 0.6 mL	1 tablespoon = 15 mL	1 cup = 240 mL
¼ teaspoon = 1.2 mL	⅛ cup = 30 mL	1 fluid ounce = 30 mL
½ teaspoon = 2.5 mL	¼ cup = 60 mL	1 ounce = 28 grams
1 teaspoon = 5 mL	½ cup = 120 mL	1 fluid pound = 500 mL
½ tablespoon = 7.5 mL	¾ cup = 175 mL	1 pound = 453 grams

© 2016, 2022, 2023
Book design © Fox Chapel Publishing
Recipes and photographs © G&R Publishing DBA CQ Products
Magnificent Meals in a Bowl Cookbook (2023) is a compilation of *Loaded Salads* (2016) and *Bold Bowls* (2022) originally published by CQ Products. This version published by Fox Chapel Publishing Company, Inc., 903 Square Street, Mount Joy, PA 17552.

ISBN 978-1-4971-0384-9

Library of Congress Control Number: 2023930333

Shutterstock photos: WS-Studio (7 bottom), Binh Thanh Bui (9 lo mein noodes), Anton Starikov (10 rice noodles), JeniFoto (56 bottom), suwijaknook6644689 (57 bottom), natali_ploskaya (93)

To learn more about the other great books from Fox Chapel Publishing, or to find a retailer near you, call toll-free 800-457-9112 or visit us at *www.FoxChapelPublishing.com*.

We are always looking for talented authors. To submit an idea, please send a brief inquiry to acquisitions@foxchapelpublishing.com.

Printed in China
First printing

Magnificent
MEALS in a BOWL
COOKBOOK

HEALTHY, FAST, EASY RECIPES WITH VEGAN-AND-KETO-FRIENDLY CHOICES

GABRIELLE GARCIA

FOX CHAPEL
PUBLISHING

17

44

71

Contents

96

104

132

Introduction

Picture that you're sitting at a dining table with a meal in front of you. You're probably imagining a plate with a knife and fork, right? But so many of our favorite foods are in bowls: salads, pasta, rice, oatmeal, the list goes on and on. Get ready to broaden your horizons! This book is chock full of recipes that are perfect for those foods you already love, plus a ton of eye-opening options that will make you love these magnificent meals in a bowl.

I started my bowl journey in college. Like most students, I had a limited budget and limited time that I needed to make count. By just loading up a salad with tons of goodies like hard-boiled eggs, chicken, or fruit, I had a filling meal that might even provide leftovers! Rice and ramen noodles could be transformed in a variety of ways. And all these options were great for taking meals on the go. I took this mindset with me through life, upgrading the ingredients and adding even more variety. Always, the goal was to be as healthy as possible without sacrificing my limited free time. Now I can pass all I've learned onto you.

Meals served in bowls have been called many names, from grain bowls and harvest bowls to protein bowls and buddha bowls. They're a great way to get in lots of veggies, healthy fats, and good protein. What I love the most is how perfect they are for customization. Having kids means one loves brussels sprouts while another hates them; with these recipes, you can easily swap out any ingredient—even in the same meal. I recommend making ingredients separately so everyone can grab the parts they want, similar to a salad bar. But you could also cook a base or protein for the week and swap it in for a similar recipe throughout the week. It's a ton of fun!

Recipes that include no meat have been labeled with either "vegetarian" or "vegan," depending on their ingredients. But you'll also find a few bonus recipes, labeled "snack." These are perfect additions to a bowl meal, can be eaten on their own, or could even be used for a sandwich. It's never been easier to prepare your meals for the week.

Whether served in individual bowls or piled into one really big one, these recipes are ideal for singles, couples, and families alike. Have fun, get creative, and eat well!

Kitchen Tools & Equipment

One of the great features of these magnificent meals is that they don't require a ton of special equipment taking up space on my counter! For the most part, the tools used throughout this book are the basics that most people keep in their kitchen. Of the few "specialty" items you'll find, once I bought them, I now use those frequently as well. It's all up to preference. Maybe you won't use a food processor every day, so it makes sense to use a traditional cutting board. However, I recommend these tools for an easy and fun experience when you're cooking.

Kitchen Basics

- Serving bowls
- Mixing bowls
- Mixing spoons
- Slotted spoon
- Kitchen knives
- Whisk
- Aluminum foil
- Parchment paper
- Baking pan
- Baking sheet
- Saucepans

Specialty Tools

- Fine-mesh strainer
- High-powered blender
- Skillet
- Mason jar
- Food processor
- Grill pan

The Anatomy of a Magnificent Meal Bowl

The four main components that make for a great meal are a grain or starch to use as the base, a smattering of protein, and an assortment of various vegetables, and a sauce. I find it's much easier to break a meal down into these components so I know how to customize—or add a little extra if I want! Throw on some fresh herbs and a crunchy element for good measure, then artfully arrange the ingredients to make them look pretty. Sauce it up with something store-bought, or make one of the many recipes for sauces, dressings, and vinaigrettes listed inside.

Vibrant flavors + contrasting textures = a delicious meal

Meal Bowl

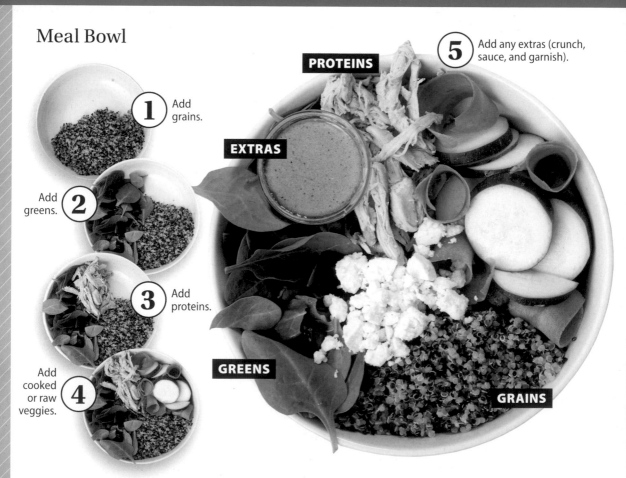

1 Add grains.

2 Add greens.

3 Add proteins.

4 Add cooked or raw veggies.

5 Add any extras (crunch, sauce, and garnish).

PROTEINS

EXTRAS

GREENS

GRAINS

Base

Whether you choose grains like rice, quinoa, or barley; a veggie like mashed potatoes or spaghetti squash; or noodles like pasta or rice noodles, cook up a batch and use it as the base for your bowl. If you go for a salad, this component might be small or nonexistent, while your greens are used as the base. It all depends on what you want to eat!

Barley is a whole grain with a mild, slightly nutty taste and chewy texture.

Chia seeds [CHEE-uh] are tiny and crunchy with a subtle flavor. When soaked in liquid, they develop a gel-like texture similar to tapioca.

Couscous [KOOS-koos] is a form of pasta made from semolina. It cooks very quickly and has a neutral flavor.

Farro [FAHR-oh] belongs to the wheat family and has a dense, chewy texture and a rich, nutty flavor.

Lo mein noodles [LOH-main] are a type of egg noodle, made using wheat flour and eggs. They have a neutral flavor.

Old-fashioned oats are flat and flakey. They absorb more water and cook faster than steel-cut oats.

Pasta comes in so many varieties, ingredients, and flavors to choose from.

Polenta [poh-LEHN-tah] is a gluten-free mush made from coarsely ground corn (cornmeal). Freshly cooked, polenta is soft and creamy. When cooled, it firms up and can be sliced and fried.

Potatoes are tubers that come in a variety of options. Russets are recommended for mashing.

Quinoa [KEEN-wah] is a gluten-free seed that is a good alternative to starchy grains. It has a delicate flavor and expands to four times its volume when cooked.

Ramen [RAH-men] are most often found as instant-style noodles. They cook quickly and come with a seasoning packet.

Rice comes in many forms and varieties and is often classified by its size (long grain, medium grain, short grain).

Rice noodles are made from rice flour and water. They have a nutty, slightly sweet taste.

Sweet potatoes are large, starchy, sweet-tasting root vegetables.

Wild rice is actually a semi-aquatic grass. It has a firm texture and toasted nut-like flavor.

Protein

Meat options include poultry, pork, beef, or seafood; for meatless meals, go for other delicious options like eggs, beans, tofu, or lentils. Try swapping out the proteins in any of these recipes—these recipes are perfect for customizing to your diet and taste preferences!

Cooked Veggies

Use more than one for a variety of flavors and colors or just stick to your favorite. Roasted, steamed, or grilled, they add healthy goodness.

Raw Veggies

Choose salad greens or reach for something with additional crunch, like carrots, radishes, or bell peppers. This adds a hit of bold freshness to your bowl. Tear or chop your favorite greens into bite-size pieces so they're easier to eat. Choose darker greens for more nutrients.

Garnish

Sprinkling fresh herbs or microgreens over your bowl just before serving looks and tastes great.

Crunch

Go simple with nuts and seeds. Or use one of the snack recipes throughout the book for crunch with a little personality.

Sauce

Go with a salad dressing, vinaigrette, or specialty sauce. Serve it on the side or pour it over the top of the bowls.

1. Wash greens and pat them dry with clean towels (or use a salad spinner) so dressings will cling well.
2. Use 1 or 2 tablespoons of dressing per 2-cup serving of salad so your ingredients won't get soggy.
3. As you prep a dressing, taste test with the greens; some that seem too strong alone will taste perfect with the other ingredients.
4. Always shake or stir your dressing before adding it to a salad.
5. Homemade dressings will stay fresh for several weeks in the refrigerator. For the best flavor, let creamy ones warm up a little before using.

Meal Planning

With the way these recipes use basic components to build a meal, they are perfect for planning meals ahead of time! When you have a batch of precooked grains, veggies, pasta, or protein waiting in the fridge or freezer, it makes meal prep faster and easier. Prepping even bits and pieces of bowl recipes can give you a jump on the week ahead. I like picking one ingredient to make in a large batch, such as chicken or wild rice, and then finding other recipes that use it! That way I have a variety of flavors throughout the week without wasting time I'd rather use elsewhere.

Do you have picky eaters in the house? No problem! When you make the ingredients ahead of time, they can leave out the Brussels sprouts or just eat sauce on their chicken. Meals in bowls are all about versatility! Everyone at the table can have a unique bowl while using the same components—it's all a matter of quantity and individual tastes. Play around with different foods and create something unique for every meal.

By prepping pieces ahead of time, I come up with all kinds of recipes and delicious variations! Giving leftovers a second chance is a bowl-maker's dream. Nobody has to know whether you planned ahead or were lucky enough to have leftovers that combined to create a really great meal.

I love these sectioned containers because some ingredients stay fresh longer when mixed at the very end.

On-the-go prep

Do you know what's even better? These recipes are perfect for on-the-go eating. Whether you're going on a picnic, taking a road trip, or need lunch for work, these salads, smoothies, and grain bowls are quick and easy to store and carry with plastic storage containers.

Keeping the sauce or dressing in a separate container keeps ingredients from getting soggy. To assure crisp veggies stay that way, keep them separate from cooked items. Same goes for crunchy toppings like peanuts.

All you have to do is choose your favorite ingredients and go!

Breakfast

Start your day right with these bowl meals.
These recipes have those classic components
associated with breakfast: oatmeal, fruit,
eggs, and bacon. Just like any recipe in
this book, these meals are super versatile,
and they can be eaten at any time of the day!

Orange-Peach Smoothie Bowls

SERVES 2 **VEGETARIAN**

INGREDIENTS

1 ½ cups
   frozen peaches
¼ frozen banana
¼ cup milk
¼ cup orange juice
¾ cup plain
   Greek yogurt

1 ½ to 2 tbsp. honey
Pinch of cinnamon
½ tsp. vanilla
Garnishes: Toasted
   almonds, granola,
   peach slices

INSTRUCTIONS

In a high-powered blender*, combine frozen peaches, frozen banana, milk, orange juice, Greek yogurt, honey, cinnamon, and vanilla. Blend on high speed, scraping down the sides often. Top with toasted almonds, granola, and peach slices.

No high-powered blender? You may need to add a bit more liquid or a little less frozen fruit.

Greens & Pineapple Smoothie Bowls

SERVES 2 **VEGETARIAN**

INGREDIENTS

10 oz. frozen mango
1 avocado, peeled
   & pitted
1 cup fresh spinach
1 tsp. vanilla
3 tbsps. milk

1 to 2 tbsps. honey
Garnishes: Avocado
   slices, unsweetened
   coconut chips,
   chia seeds

INSTRUCTIONS

In a high-powered blender*, combine frozen mango, avocado, spinach, vanilla, milk, and honey. Blend on low speed; increase to high, scraping down the sides often. It will be thick! Top with avocado slices, unsweetened coconut chips, and chia seeds.

Mixed Fruit Smoothie Bowls

SERVES 3   VEGETARIAN

INGREDIENTS

1 cup frozen acai
1 banana
⅓ cup pineapple
  chunks
1 ¼ cups frozen
  cherry-berry blend

¼ cup plain
  Greek yogurt
¼ cup milk
1 tbsp. honey
Garnishes: Fresh
  berries, cherries,
  granola, walnuts

INSTRUCTIONS

In a high-powered blender*, combine frozen acai, banana, pineapple chunks, frozen cherry-berry blend, Greek yogurt, milk, and honey. Process until smooth, scraping down the sides often. Divide among serving bowls. Top with berries, cherries, granola, and walnuts.

*No high-powered blender? You may need to add a bit more liquid or a little less frozen fruit.

PB & Banana Smoothie Bowls

SERVES 2   VEGETARIAN

INGREDIENTS

3 frozen ripe bananas
3 tbsps. creamy
  peanut butter
¾ cup plain
  Greek yogurt
¾ tsp. vanilla

½ cup milk
Garnishes: Banana
  slices, chocolate
  chips, peanuts,
  honey, cinnamon

INSTRUCTIONS

In a high-powered blender*, combine frozen bananas, peanut butter, Greek yogurt, vanilla, and milk. Process until smooth and creamy, scraping down the sides often. Transfer the mixture to serving bowls and top with banana slices, chocolate chips, peanuts, honey, and cinnamon.

Chocolate Toasted Quinoa

SERVES 2 VEGETARIAN

INGREDIENTS

1 cup quinoa
2 cups milk
Pinch of sea salt
2 to 2½ tbsps.
   unsweetened
   cocoa powder

2 to 3 tbsps.
   coconut sugar
½ tsp. vanilla
Garnishes: Milk, dark
   chocolate chunks,
   fresh fruit

INSTRUCTIONS

Pour quinoa into a hot saucepan and toast for a couple of minutes, shaking saucepan often. Pour in milk and sea salt. Bring to a boil, reduce heat to low, and simmer uncovered 15 to 20 minutes or to the texture you like, stirring occasionally.

Remove from the heat and stir in cocoa powder, coconut sugar, and vanilla; divide among bowls. Top with milk, dark chocolate chunks, and fresh fruit.

Cozy Warm Chia

SERVES 2 VEGETARIAN

INGREDIENTS

6 tbsps. chia seeds
2 cups milk
2 to 3 tbsps. honey or
   pure maple syrup
2 tsps. vanilla

Pinch of salt
Garnishes:
   Cherries, almonds,
   sesame seeds,
   and cinnamon

INSTRUCTIONS

In a saucepan, combine chia seeds and milk; bring to a low boil and cook for 3 to 5 minutes, until it begins to thicken. Remove from the heat and stir in honey, vanilla, and salt; divide among bowls and top with cherries, almonds, sesame seeds, and cinnamon.

Steel-Cut PB&J

SERVES 2 `VEGETARIAN`

INGREDIENTS

- ½ cup steel-cut oats (enough for 2 servings)
- ½ cup milk
- 1 tbsp. pure maple syrup or agave
- ½ tsp. cinnamon
- ¼ cup dried cranberries
- Garnishes: Thin apple slices, peanut butter, strawberry jam (or your favorite flavor), peanuts

INSTRUCTIONS

In a saucepan, prepare steel-cut oats according to package directions to make 2 servings. Once cooked, stir in milk. Bring to a slow boil then simmer for several minutes until creamy and most of the liquid has absorbed, stirring often. Remove from the heat and stir in maple syrup, cinnamon, and dried cranberries; divide among bowls. Top with apple slices, a dollop of peanut butter, some strawberry jam, and a few peanuts.

Easy Turmeric Oatmeal

SERVES 2 `VEGETARIAN`

INGREDIENTS

- 2 cups milk
- 2 tsps. pure maple syrup
- 1 tsp. ground turmeric
- ½ tsp. ground cinnamon
- ¼ tsp. ground ginger
- ½ tsp. vanilla
- Pinch of black pepper
- 1 cup old-fashioned oats
- Garnishes: Plain Greek yogurt, frozen mixed fruit, mint leaves, powdered sugar

INSTRUCTIONS

In a small saucepan, combine milk, maple syrup, turmeric, cinnamon, ginger, vanilla, and black pepper; bring to a boil. Stir in old-fashioned oats; reduce heat and simmer for 5 to 8 minutes, until thickened, stirring occasionally. Divide among bowls and top with Greek yogurt, frozen mixed fruit, mint leaves, and a dusting of powdered sugar.

Bacon, Eggs & Barley
with Creamy Dijonnaise

SERVES 4

MEAL

- 2 cups barley (enough for 4 servings)
- 4 cups vegetable broth
- 8 bacon strips
- 1 bunch asparagus
- 2½ cups grape tomatoes
- Salt and black pepper, to taste
- 4 eggs
- 1 tbsp. apple cider vinegar
- Pepita seeds, roasted, to taste
- Red pepper flakes, to taste

SAUCE

- ½ cup sour cream
- ¼ cup mayonnaise
- 1 tsp. Dijon mustard
- ¼ cup fresh lemon juice
- Salt and black pepper, to taste

INSTRUCTIONS

1 Make the **Creamy Dijonnaise**. Stir together sour cream, mayo, mustard, fresh lemon juice, salt, and black pepper. Refrigerate until needed.

2 Cook barley according to package directions to make 4 servings, using vegetable broth as the cooking liquid.

3 Preheat the oven to 400°F. Lay bacon slices on a foil-lined baking pan. Bake for 18 to 20 minutes or until done.

4 While bacon is cooking, cut asparagus into bite-size pieces and toss onto a rimmed baking pan. Add grape tomatoes. Drizzle with olive oil and sprinkle generously with salt and black pepper. Roast at 400°F for 10 to 15 minutes, until asparagus is crisp-tender.

5 Divide barley, bacon, and roasted veggies among serving bowls.

6 Crack 1 egg into a fine-mesh strainer set over a small bowl. Let drain for 30 seconds to remove excess liquid. Pour the egg from the strainer into a second small bowl. Repeat with 3 more eggs, putting each into a separate bowl. Fill a medium saucepan with 4" of water; bring to a boil. Reduce heat to low and add apple cider vinegar. One at a time, tip the eggs into the barely simmering water and cook for 3 minutes. Remove with a slotted spoon. Add to the serving bowls.

7 Top with roasted pepitas. If desired, add red pepper flakes for spicy pepitas.

8 Serve with Creamy Dijonnaise.

Bacon & Eggs with Kale
with Bacon-Maple Vinaigrette

SERVES 4

SALAD

- 4 eggs
- 4 cups sourdough bread, cubed
- ¼ cup butter
- 1 tsp. minced garlic
- 1 tbsp. dried oregano
- 1 tbsp. dried cilantro
- 4 cups kale leaves, chopped
- 2 cups baby spinach
- 6 bacon strips (reserve drippings)

VINAIGRETTE

- 3 tbsps. pure maple syrup
- 2 tbsps. apple cider vinegar
- ½ tsp. garlic, minced
- ½ tsp. Dijon mustard
- ¼ tsp. salt
- ¼ tsp. black pepper
- ¼ cup bacon drippings

INSTRUCTIONS

1 Place eggs in a saucepan of cold water and bring to a boil; boil gently for 1 minute. Cover pan, remove from heat, and let stand about 14 minutes. Cool the eggs in ice water for a few minutes, then peel and return to water until completely cool. Slice and set aside.

2 Preheat the oven to 400°F. To make croutons, spread bread cubes on a rimmed baking sheet and bake for 10 minutes, until lightly browned. Meanwhile, melt the butter in a small saucepan; whisk in the garlic, oregano, and cilantro. Pour butter mixture over croutons and toss well; bake 5 to 10 minutes longer.

3 In a large bowl, combine the kale and spinach, then refrigerate until needed.

4 Cook the bacon in a skillet over medium-high heat until crisp; rest on paper towels. Measure ¼ cup of the reserved drippings and keep warm.

5 Prepare the **Maple-Bacon Vinaigrette** by whisking together the maple syrup, apple cider vinegar, garlic, mustard, salt, and pepper. Slowly whisk in the warm bacon drippings until well blended.

6 Toss the kale mixture with some of the vinaigrette and crumble the bacon on top. Add the prepped croutons and eggs and serve with the remaining dressing.

This salad is good enough to eat for breakfast, lunch, or dinner!

Combo
Salads

What's a combo salad? It's all the greens
you love combined with a meat! Whether
it's chicken, beef, pork, or seafood, there are
a variety of flavors and styles for the meat-
lovers in your family. But if you don't eat
meat or other products made from animals,
don't be deterred! By swapping
one protein for another, these salads
can be just as delicious.

Cran-Chicken & Almonds
with Raspberry Vinaigrette

SERVES 4

SALAD

½ cup sliced almonds

1 tbsp. water

2 tbsps. sugar

8 cups romaine, torn

¾ cup dried
    sweetened cranberries

2 cups grilled chicken strips

Garnish: Crumbled
    blue cheese

VINAIGRETTE

1 cup fresh raspberries

2 tbsps. sugar

½ cup apple cider vinegar

¼ cup grapeseed oil

1½ tbsps. sweet onion, grated

1 tbsp. honey

½ tsp. salt

INSTRUCTIONS

1 Combine almonds and sugar in a nonstick skillet over medium heat. When skillet is hot, add water; cook and stir until nuts are lightly browned and liquid evaporates. Dump onto waxed paper and toss with more sugar and a sprinkling of sea salt; let cool.

2 To make a **Raspberry Vinaigrette**, toss raspberries, sugar, apple cider vinegar, grapeseed oil, sweet onion, honey, and salt into a blender and process well.

3 Combine romaine, cranberries, chicken strips, some crumbled blue cheese, and the cooled almonds. Serve with the vinaigrette.

Pastrami & Rye Panzanella
with Red Wine Vinaigrette

SERVES 4

SALAD

½ cup red onion, thinly sliced

3 cups light rye bread, cubed

1 lb. tomatoes, seeded & roughly diced

¼ tsp. salt

2 mini cucumbers (3 oz. each), thinly sliced

2 celery ribs, sliced

4 oz. sliced pastrami, chopped

¾ cup fresh basil, chopped

Caraway seeds

VINAIGRETTE

1 tsp. minced garlic

¼ tsp. salt

¼ cup grapeseed oil

1 tbsp. red wine vinegar

INSTRUCTIONS

1 To make the **Red Wine Vinaigrette**, mash the garlic and salt together in a bowl, then whisk in the other ingredients until well blended; set aside.

2 For the salad, soak onion slices in a bowl of cold water for 10 minutes; drain and repeat twice. Pat dry and set aside.

3 Preheat the oven to 450°F. Spread the bread cubes on a rimmed baking sheet and bake for 6 to 8 minutes or until edges are crisp and golden brown. Let cool.

4 In a large bowl, toss the toasted bread cubes, tomatoes, and salt together until combined. Add the cucumbers, celery, pastrami, basil, and soaked onion slices.

5 Drizzle the prepared vinaigrette over the salad and toss well. Sprinkle with caraway seeds and enjoy!

Layered Taco Salad
with Creamy Taco Dressing

SERVES 8

SALAD

- 1½ lbs. boneless & skinless chicken breasts, trimmed to ½" thickness
- 1½ to 2 tbsps. taco seasoning mix
- 2 tbsps. canola oil
- 2 tbsps. butter
- 1½ cups frozen corn, thawed
- 1 large head green leaf lettuce, shredded
- 3 plum tomatoes, diced
- 1 avocado, peeled, pitted & diced
- 3 scallions, sliced
- ½ to 1 cup crumbled Cotija or shredded Pepper Jack cheese
- Garnishes: Broken tortilla chips, fresh cilantro

DRESSING

- ¾ cup bottled ranch dressing
- ¼ cup salsa
- 3 tbsps. minced fresh cilantro

INSTRUCTIONS

1 Whisk the **Creamy Taco Dressing** ingredients together and chill for later use.

2 For the salad, coat chicken with taco seasoning. Combine oil and butter in a skillet over medium-high heat, and cook the chicken until browned, about 4 minutes per side. Let cool 10 minutes, then dice.

3 Toss the corn into the same skillet, stirring until well coated. Cook over medium heat until warm and slightly browned, about 3 minutes; set aside.

4 In a large glass bowl, layer half the lettuce and most of the tomatoes, corn, chicken, avocado, and onions. Top with the remaining lettuce and cheese; garnish with any remaining salad ingredients plus some chips and cilantro.

5 Drizzle the chilled dressing over the salad or serve it on the side.

French Dressing

INGREDIENTS

6-ounce can tomato paste
⅓ to ½ cup sugar
½ cup olive oil
¼ cup white vinegar
¼ cup lemon juice
½ medium onion, grated
¼ tsp. Worcestershire sauce
½ tsp. salt
½ tsp. paprika
½ tsp. garlic, minced

INSTRUCTIONS

In a shaker jar, combine ingredients. Cover and shake well.
Store in the refrigerator.

Caribbean Turkey Salad
with Honey-Mustard Dressing

SERVES 4

SALAD

- 1 lb. boneless & skinless turkey breast fillets
- ½ cup teriyaki marinade sauce
- 2 tomatoes, seeded & chopped
- ½ cup onion, chopped
- 2 tsps. jalapeño peppers, minced
- 2 tsps. fresh cilantro, chopped
- ¼ tsp. salt
- 8 cups salad greens, chopped
- 8-ounce can pineapple tidbits, drained
- Garnish: Broken corn tortilla chips

DRESSING

- ¼ cup Dijon mustard
- ¼ cup honey
- 1½ tbsps. sugar
- 1½ tbsps. apple cider vinegar
- 1 tbsp. vegetable oil
- 1½ tsps. lime juice

INSTRUCTIONS

1 Whisk the dressing ingredients together and set aside for later use.

2 Combine the turkey and teriyaki sauce in a large bowl; cover and marinate in the refrigerator for at least 2 hours.

3 While turkey is marinating, mix the tomatoes, onion, jalapeños, cilantro, and salt in a small bowl; cover and chill until serving.

4 Discard the marinade and grill the turkey over medium-high heat until fully cooked, 5 to 8 minutes per side. Let rest a few minutes, then slice into strips.

5 To assemble the salad, arrange greens on serving bowls and top with some of the chilled tomato mixture, pineapple, turkey slices, and chips. Drizzle with the prepared dressing and serve immediately.

Thousand Island Dressing

INGREDIENTS

1 cup mayo

¼ cup ketchup

2 tbsps. rice vinegar

¼ tsp. salt

Dash of black pepper

4 tsps. sugar

4 tsps. sweet pickle relish

4 tsps. white onion, finely minced

INSTRUCTIONS

In a bowl, stir ingredients until well combined. Chill a few hours, stirring occasionally to help sugar dissolve. Store in the refrigerator.

Chicken Fajita Salad
with Lime & Cilantro Vinaigrette

SERVES 4

SALAD

1 ½ to 2 tbsps. fresh lime juice

1 ½ tbsps. olive oil

1 tsp. garlic, minced

½ tsp. salt

½ tsp. ground cumin

½ tsp. chili powder

½ jalapeño pepper, seeded & minced

2 tbsps. fresh cilantro, chopped

1 lb. boneless & skinless chicken
   breasts, cut into strips

2 tbsps. canola oil

½ onion, thinly sliced

1 zucchini, cut into strips

1 green bell pepper, seeded & sliced

8 to 10 cups romaine or green leaf
   lettuce, chopped

1 tomato, sliced

1 avocado, peeled, pitted & sliced

Garnish: Tortilla strips

VINAIGRETTE

1 ½ to 2 tbsps. fresh lime juice

¼ cup fresh cilantro

2 tbsps. canola oil

½ tsp. garlic, minced

Salt and black pepper, to taste

INSTRUCTIONS

1 Insert the **Lime & Cilantro Vinaigrette** ingredients into a blender or food processor and process until smooth; set aside.

2 For the salad, mix the lime juice, olive oil, garlic, salt, cumin, chili powder, jalapeño, and cilantro in a big bowl. Add the chicken, toss well, and let marinate at room temperature for 30 minutes.

3 In a large deep skillet, heat 1 tbsp. canola oil and sauté the chicken strips until cooked through, turning often; transfer to a bowl and set aside.

4 Heat 1 tbsp. canola oil in the same skillet and add the onion, zucchini, and bell pepper. Sauté until tender, 2 to 3 minutes. Stir chicken and juices back into skillet and cook until coated and heated through.

5 Divide the lettuce, tomato, and avocado among serving bowls and top with the cooked chicken mixture. Sprinkle with tortilla strips and serve with the set-aside vinaigrette.

Cheeseburger & Fries Salad
with Cowboy Dressing

SERVES 4

SALAD

1 lb. frozen steak fries, partially thawed

½ tsp. smoked paprika

¼ tsp. cayenne pepper

Salt and black pepper, to taste

1 lb. lean ground beef

1 cup onion, diced

⅔ cup ketchup

2 tsps. Worcestershire sauce

2 tbsps. yellow mustard

8 cups green leaf lettuce, torn

1 cup grape tomatoes, halved

1 cup shredded cheddar cheese

Garnish: Sliced scallions

DRESSING

½ cup olive oil

¼ cup white wine vinegar

1 tsp. sugar

¼ cup ketchup

1 tsp. Worcestershire sauce

Salt and black pepper, to taste

INSTRUCTIONS

1 Whisk the **Cowboy Dressing** ingredients until well blended; set aside.

2 For the salad, put the fries in a big bowl and sprinkle with the paprika, cayenne pepper, salt, and black pepper; toss well. Bake as directed on the package.

3 While the fries bake, brown the ground beef and onion in a skillet over medium heat until cooked through and crumbly; drain. Stir in the ketchup, Worcestershire sauce, and mustard, cooking until heated through. Season with salt and black pepper and remove from heat.

4 Divide the lettuce among serving dishes and top evenly with the beef, fries, tomatoes, cheese, and onions. Drizzle salads with the set-aside dressing or serve it on the side.

Creamy Russian Dressing

INGREDIENTS

1 tbsp. onion, minced

½ tsp. salt

1 cup mayo

¼ cup chili sauce

3 to 4 tsps. creamy horseradish

1 tsp. hot sauce

1 tsp. Worcestershire sauce

¼ tsp. paprika

INSTRUCTIONS

In a bowl, mash together onion and salt. Add the rest of the ingredients; whisk well. Store in the refrigerator.

Pork & Orange Chop Salad

SERVES 4

INGREDIENTS

1 lb. pork tenderloin, cut into
  ½" pieces

2½ tsps. Szechwan seasoning mix

½ tsp. salt

1 tbsp. olive oil

2 oranges, peeled

1 cup English cucumber, chopped

¼ cup fresh cilantro, chopped

½ cup bottled sesame-
  ginger dressing

1 head romaine lettuce, chopped

3 cups shredded coleslaw

½ cup wasabi & soy sauce-
  flavored almonds

INSTRUCTIONS

1 Toss the pork pieces with seasoning and salt until well coated. Heat oil in a large skillet over medium-high heat and cook the pork 6 to 9 minutes or until lightly browned and cooked through, turning often.

2 Slice the oranges and cut them into chunks.

3 Toss the oranges, cucumber, and cilantro into a large bowl with the bottled dressing; let marinate about 5 minutes. Add the lettuce, coleslaw mix, and pork, then toss gently.

4 Sprinkle with almonds and serve immediately.

This salad also tastes great using strips of seasoned grilled chicken in place of the breaded version.

Dixie Chicken, Broccoli & Grapes
with Honey-Mustard Vinaigrette

SERVES 4

SALAD

1 egg, lightly beaten

1½ tbsps. water

(4) 4-ounce chicken cutlets, ¼" to ½" thick

⅔ cup seasoned breadcrumbs

8 cups fresh spinach or leaf lettuce

1½ cups fresh broccoli florets

1 cup red or green grapes, halved

¼ cup honey-roasted almonds

VINAIGRETTE

3½ tbsps. apple cider vinegar

3 tbsps. honey

1½ tsps. Dijon mustard

¼ cup olive oil

¼ tsp. salt

⅛ tsp. black pepper

INSTRUCTIONS

1 Preheat the oven to 425°F. Whisk together the egg and water. Dip the chicken in egg mixture and then dredge in breadcrumbs until well coated. Set the cutlets on a greased foil-lined baking sheet and bake for 15 minutes or until chicken is lightly browned and fully cooked.

2 While chicken is cooking, combine the **Honey-Mustard Vinaigrette** ingredients in a jar with a tight-fitting lid. Cover and shake well; set aside.

3 To assemble the salad, divide the greens, broccoli, and grapes among serving bowls. Slice the chicken and arrange some on top of each salad. Sprinkle with almonds and serve with the set-aside vinaigrette.

Ranch Dressing

INGREDIENTS

½ cup sour cream	1½ tsps. dill weed
½ cup mayonnaise	½ tsp. garlic powder
½ cup buttermilk	⅛ tsp. black pepper
1½ tsps. fresh chives, chopped	¼ tsp. onion powder
	¼ tsp. white vinegar
1½ tsps. parsley	¼ tsp. salt

INSTRUCTIONS

In a bowl, whisk together sour cream, mayo, and buttermilk. Add the rest of the ingredients; mix well. Chill a few hours before using. Store in the refrigerator.

Steak & Mushroom Salad
with Creamy Buttermilk Dressing

SERVES 4

SALAD

2 tsps. canola oil

(2) ¾ lb. New York strip steaks

Salt and black pepper, to taste

8 oz. baby bella mushrooms, sliced

6 to 8 cups arugula

2 scallions, sliced

¼ cup fresh dill weed, snipped

1 cup smoked gouda cheese, cubed

DRESSING

⅓ cup mayonnaise

3 tbsps. buttermilk

2 tsps. lemon juice

1 tsp. garlic, minced

2 tbsps. canola or grapeseed oil

¼ tsp. salt

2 tbsps. fresh dill weed, snipped
(optional)

INSTRUCTIONS

1 Whisk the **Creamy Buttermilk Dressing** ingredients together until well mixed. Set aside to let flavors blend.

2 For the salad, heat the oil in a heavy skillet over medium-high heat. Season the steak with salt and pepper, then add to skillet and sear well on both sides. Reduce heat to medium, partially cover the skillet, and fry to desired doneness, 3 to 7 minutes per side. Remove to a plate and let rest 5 minutes before slicing into strips.

3 While steak is cooking, season the mushrooms with salt and pepper and sauté them in the same skillet over medium heat about 5 minutes or until browned and tender, stirring often; remove from heat.

4 In a big bowl, toss the arugula with the onions and dill. Divide among serving bowls and top evenly with steak slices, mushrooms, and cheese. Serve promptly with the dressing.

Italian Dressing

INGREDIENTS

1 tsp. garlic salt

1 tsp. onion powder

1 tsp. dried parsley

1 tsp. sugar

2 tsps. dried oregano

½ tsp. dried basil

½ tsp. black pepper

Pinch of dried thyme

Pinch of celery salt

⅛ tsp. red pepper flakes (optional)

¼ cup white vinegar

⅔ cup canola oil

2 tbsps. water

INSTRUCTIONS

In a shaker jar, mix garlic salt, onion powder, parsley, sugar, oregano, basil, black pepper, thyme, celery salt, and red pepper flakes. Add white vinegar; cover, shake, and let stand at least 5 minutes. Add canola oil and water and shake vigorously. Store in the refrigerator.

Salmon & Roasted Veggies
with Garlic Vinaigrette

SERVES 4

SALAD

- 6 cups peeled, cubed root vegetables (sweet and white potatoes, turnips, carrots, or beets)
- 1 tbsp. olive oil
- Salt and black pepper, to taste
- 8 oz. frozen salmon fillets, thawed
- Garlic salt, to taste
- 8 cups mixed salad greens
- 2 scallions, sliced

VINAIGRETTE

- 2 tbsps. olive oil
- 2 tbsps. red wine vinegar
- 1 tbsp. garlic, minced
- 1 tsp. whole-grain mustard
- 1 tsp. anchovy paste
- ¼ tsp. salt
- ¼ tsp. black pepper
- ¼ tsp. sugar

INSTRUCTIONS

1 Whisk the **Garlic Vinaigrette** ingredients together until well blended and set aside.

2 Preheat the oven to 450°F and line a large, rimmed baking sheet with greased foil. In a large bowl, toss the vegetables with oil and season with salt and pepper. Spread in a single layer on the prepped pan and roast for 20 to 25 minutes, stirring once, until tender and golden brown.

3 While veggies are cooking, brush the salmon with oil and sprinkle with garlic salt and pepper. Grill over medium-high heat until salmon is opaque and flakes easily with a fork. Let rest a few minutes, then break into chunks.

4 Combine the roasted veggies, salmon, and onions with 2 tbsps. of the vinaigrette and toss lightly. Divide the greens among serving bowls and top with some of the vegetable mixture. Serve promptly with the remaining vinaigrette.

Buffaloed Chicken Salad
with Easy Blue Cheese Dressing

SERVES 4

SALAD

2 tbsps. flour

¼ tsp. salt

⅛ tsp. black pepper

1 lb. boneless & skinless chicken breasts, cut into ¾" pieces

2 tbsps. olive oil

2 tbsps. hot sauce

2 tsps. red wine vinegar

8 cups romaine lettuce, chopped

3 large carrots, peeled & chopped

3 celery ribs, sliced

1 cucumber, peeled, seeded & chopped

Garnish: Crumbled blue cheese

DRESSING

½ cup crumbled blue cheese

6 tbsps. buttermilk

2 tsps. red wine vinegar

INSTRUCTIONS

1 Mix the **Easy Blue Cheese Dressing** ingredients together and set aside.

2 For the salad, mix the flour, salt, and pepper in a medium bowl and add the chicken pieces; toss until well coated. Heat the oil in a large skillet over medium-high heat and cook the chicken for 6 to 7 minutes or until fully cooked and golden brown on all sides.

3 Stir in the hot sauce and vinegar and cook about 1 minute longer, until chicken is glazed and sauce is warm.

4 In a big bowl, toss the lettuce with the carrots, celery, and cucumber. Drizzle with the prepped dressing and toss again.

5 Divide the salad among serving bowls and top evenly with chicken and a sprinkling of blue cheese.

Classic Blue Cheese Dressing

INGREDIENTS

2½ oz. blue cheese

3 tbsps. buttermilk

3 tbsps. sour cream

2 tbsps. mayonnaise,

2 tsps. white wine vinegar

¼ tsp. sugar

¼ tsp. garlic powder

Salt and black pepper, to taste

INSTRUCTIONS

Crumble blue cheese into a bowl and stir in the rest of the ingredients. Store in the refrigerator.

Asian Deli Chicken Salad

SERVES 2

INGREDIENTS

½ to ¾ oz. rice noodles, uncooked

2 cups mixed spring greens
   or arugula

2 cups shredded cabbage or
   coleslaw mix

⅔ cup carrot, shredded

½ cup red onion, sliced

½ cup edamame, shelled

4 to 6 oz. deli-style grilled
   chicken strips

2 fresh mandarin oranges ("cuties"),
   peeled & sliced

¼ cup walnuts, coarsely chopped

Bottled ginger dressing (I used a
   lemon-ginger-sesame vinaigrette)

INSTRUCTIONS

1 Cook the noodles in boiling water according to package directions.
Drain and rinse in cold water.

2 In a big bowl, toss the greens, cabbage, carrot, onion, edamame, and
cold noodles until well combined.

3 Divide the mixture among serving bowls and top with chicken strips,
orange pieces, and walnuts.

4 Serve with a side of the bottled dressing.

*Well-drained, canned mandarin oranges
may be substituted for the fresh ones.*

Mango Salsa Chicken Salad
with Chipotle-Lime Vinaigrette

SERVES 6

SALAD

1 mango, peeled, seeded & diced
2 plum tomatoes, chopped
½ onion, finely chopped
1 jalapeño pepper, seeded & chopped
¼ cup fresh cilantro, chopped
2½ tbsps. lime juice
8 cups baby spinach
2 cups shredded broccoli slaw
2 cups cooked chicken, diced
1 cup bell pepper, any color, diced

2 tbsps. dried & sweetened cranberries
2 tbsps. pecans, chopped
Garnish: Crumbled blue cheese

VINAIGRETTE

¾ cup bottled zesty lime vinaigrette
(I used Kraft)
3 tbsps. sugar
Generous ¼ tsp. chipotle chile powder
Generous ¼ tsp. ground cumin

INSTRUCTIONS

1 Whisk together the **Chipotle-Lime Vinaigrette** ingredients and set aside.

2 Make the salsa by mixing the mango, tomatoes, onion, jalapeño, cilantro, and lime juice in a big bowl; let marinate at least 5 minutes.

3 For the salad, toss the spinach, coleslaw mix, chicken, bell pepper, cranberries, and pecans into a big bowl and mix lightly.

4 Just before serving, divide the salad mixture among serving bowls and top with some of the mango salsa and blue cheese. Drizzle with the set-aside vinaigrette or serve it on the side.

Replace the crumbled blue cheese with diced Monterey Jack cheese for added flavor, protein, and fun.

Gingered Beef Salad
with Asian Ginger Vinaigrette

SERVES 5

SALAD

- ½ lb. roast beef, cooked & shredded
- 6 red radishes, thinly sliced
- 8 cups mixed salad greens or baby spinach
- ¼ cup fresh cilantro, chopped
- ¼ cup fresh mint, chopped
- 1 cup chow mein noodles

VINAIGRETTE

- 2 tbsps. rice vinegar
- 2 tbsps. Asian fish sauce
- 2 tbsps. canola oil
- 1½ tbsps. fresh ginger, minced
- 1 tbsp. sugar

INSTRUCTIONS

1 To make the **Asian Ginger Vinaigrette**, whisk together rice vinegar, Asian fish sauce, and canola oil in a large bowl. Add ginger and sugar; mix vigorously.

2 Add roast beef (warm or cold), red radishes, salad greens, cilantro, and fresh mint to the bowl of dressing and toss well. Top with chow mein noodles and serve immediately.

Chicken Bruschetta Salad
with Lemon Vinaigrette

SERVES 5 `SNACK`

SALAD

10 French bread slices, 1" thick

Garlic salt, to taste

2 lbs. fresh tomatoes, chopped

3 cups rotisserie
   chicken, chopped

1 English cucumber, sliced

½ cup fresh parsley, chopped

¼ cup scallions, sliced

¼ cup fresh basil, chopped

Garnish: Crumbled feta cheese

VINAIGRETTE

2 tsps. lemon zest

2 tbsps. lemon juice

2 tbsps. olive oil

1 tsp. salt

½ tsp. black pepper

INSTRUCTIONS

1 Brush both sides of 10 French bread slices with olive oil and sprinkle with garlic salt; bake at 425°F until golden brown, turning once (or grill 1 to 2 minutes per side). Let cool.

2 In a large bowl, whisk together lemon zest, lemon juice, olive oil, salt, and black pepper for **Lemon Vinaigrette**.

3 Add fresh tomatoes, rotisserie chicken, English cucumber, fresh parsley, scallions, and fresh basil. Toss well and let stand about 10 minutes. Serve over prepped garlic bread and sprinkle with crumbled feta cheese.

Chopped Apple & Ham
with Creamy Parmesan Dressing

SERVES 5

SALAD

- ½ cup pecans, chopped
- 8 cups green and red leaf lettuce, torn
- 2 cups kale, torn & stems removed
- 1 Pink Lady apple, cored & cubed
- ½ cup red radishes, chopped
- ½ cup red bell pepper, diced
- 2 cups smoked ham steak, cut into bite-size strips

DRESSING

- ½ cup plain Greek yogurt
- ¼ cup grated Parmesan cheese
- 3 tbsps. mayonnaise
- 2 tbsps. apple cider vinegar
- 1 ½ tsps. dried tarragon
- ½ tsp. black pepper
- ¼ tsp. salt

INSTRUCTIONS

1 Toast the pecans in a dry skillet over medium heat for 6 to 8 minutes or until fragrant and golden. Let cool.

2 In a big bowl, combine the lettuce, kale, apple, radishes, bell pepper, ham strips, and prepped pecans; toss well.

3 Whisk the **Creamy Parmesan Dressing** ingredients together until well blended.

4 To assemble, divide the salad mixture among serving bowls and drizzle with the dressing just before serving.

Southwestern Shrimp Salad
with Creamy Avocado Dressing

SERVES 4

SALAD

- 1 tsp. chili powder
- ¾ tsp. ground cumin
- ¾ tsp. garlic powder
- 1 tsp. salt
- 1 lb. frozen cooked shrimp, peeled, deveined & thawed
- 1 tbsp. olive oil
- ½ cup black beans, drained & rinsed
- 6 cups romaine lettuce, chopped
- 1 cup bell pepper, chopped (I used red & yellow)
- ½ cup onion, finely chopped
- Garnishes: Tortilla strips, grape tomatoes, sliced black olives (optional)

DRESSING

- ½ ripe avocado, peeled, pitted & sliced
- ¼ cup sour cream
- 3 tbsps. mayonnaise
- 1 jalapeño, seeded & chopped
- ½ to 1 cup fresh cilantro leaves and stems
- 1 tbsp. lime juice
- 2 to 3 tbsps. water
- Salt and black pepper, to taste

INSTRUCTIONS

1 For the **Creamy Avocado Dressing**, combine avocado, sour cream, mayonnaise, jalapeño, cilantro, and lime juice in a food processor and pulse until smooth. Add the water, 1 tbsp. at a time, and process to desired consistency. Season with salt and pepper and set aside.

2 For the salad, mix the chili powder, cumin, garlic powder, and salt in a medium bowl; remove 1 tsp. of the mixture and set it aside. Add shrimp to the bowl with the remainder and toss to coat well.

3 Heat the oil in a large skillet over medium-high heat; add shrimp and cook just until browned and heated through, 1 to 2 minutes per side. (If using raw shrimp, cook slightly longer, until opaque.) Transfer shrimp to a plate.

4 Toss the beans with the set-aside spice mixture and sauté in the same skillet until heated through.

5 Combine the lettuce, bell pepper, and onion in a large bowl. Top with the shrimp, beans, and tortilla strips, adding a few tomatoes and black olives, if you'd like. Serve promptly with the dressing.

Strawberry-Avocado Greens
with Bacon-Poppy Seed Dressing

SERVES 4

SALAD

6 to 8 cups baby spinach or
   kale, chopped

2 cups fresh strawberries, sliced

1 avocado, peeled & sliced

DRESSING

4 bacon strips

½ cup mayonnaise

2 tbsps. sugar

2 tbsps. white vinegar

½ tsp. poppy seeds

INSTRUCTIONS

1 To make the **Bacon-Poppy Seed Dressing**, cook
bacon strips in a skillet over medium heat until
crisp; drain on paper towels. Discard the drippings
and crumble the bacon into a small bowl. Add
mayonnaise, sugar, white vinegar, and poppy seeds
to the bowl and whisk well. Season with salt and
black pepper.

2 Place baby spinach into a big bowl and add
strawberries and avocado. Toss the salad mixture
with the prepped dressing before serving.

Light Chef's Salad
with Light Creamy Dressing

SERVES 4

SALAD

- 6 to 8 cups Boston lettuce
- 2 cups roasted turkey, sliced
- 1 avocado, diced
- ½ cup radishes, sliced
- 2 cucumbers, sliced
- 3 large carrots, julienned
- 2 cups grape tomatoes
- Alfalfa sprouts, to taste
- 4 hard-boiled eggs, sliced
- 1 cup Monterey Jack cheese, sliced

DRESSING

- ⅓ cup low-fat buttermilk
- ⅓ cup sour cream
- 1 to 2 tbsps. apple cider vinegar
- 1 tbsp. honey

INSTRUCTIONS

Mix ingredients for **Light Creamy Dressing**. Tear up Boston lettuce and divide among serving bowls. Top with roasted turkey, avocado, radishes, cucumbers, carrots, tomatoes, alfalfa sprouts, hard-boiled eggs, and strips of Monterey Jack cheese. Season as desired and serve with the dressing.

Caesar with Grilled Shrimp
with Caesar Dressing

SERVES 4

SALAD

- 1 lb. large raw shrimp, peeled & deveined
- 1 head romaine lettuce, torn
- Italian-style croutons, to taste

DRESSING

- ½ cup mayonnaise
- ⅓ cup grated Parmesan cheese
- ¼ cup lemon juice
- 2 tbsps. olive oil
- 1 tsp. Worcestershire sauce
- 1 tsp. anchovy paste
- 1 tsp. garlic, minced
- Salt and black pepper, to taste

INSTRUCTIONS

Whisk together ingredients for **Caesar Dressing**. Brush raw shrimp with olive oil; grill over medium-high heat about 2½ minutes per side, until pink and opaque. Toss romaine lettuce with the shrimp and the dressing, then sprinkle with croutons.

BBQ Chicken Cobb
with Herbed Buttermilk Dressing

SERVES 4

SALAD

2 boneless &
   skinless chicken
   breast halves
6 to 8 cups romaine
   lettuce, torn
4 hard-boiled
   eggs, chopped
½ cup bacon crumbles
1 lb. tomatoes, diced
1 avocado, diced
½ cup scallions, sliced
1 cup cheddar
   cheese, cubed

DRESSING

½ cup buttermilk
¼ cup plain
   Greek yogurt
¼ cup sour cream
½ tsp. dried dill weed
½ tsp. parsley
¼ tsp. garlic powder
¼ tsp. onion powder
Salt and black pepper
   to taste

INSTRUCTIONS

Mix ingredients for **Herbed Buttermilk Dressing**. Grill chicken breast halves; cool, dice, and toss with barbecue sauce. Top romaine lettuce with prepared chicken, chopped hard-boiled eggs, bacon crumbles, tomatoes, avocado, scallions, and cheddar cheese. Drizzle with dressing.

Fruited Chicken Salad

SERVES 6 **SNACK**

INGREDIENTS

2 cups grilled chicken breast, diced
1 apple, chopped
½ cup dried, sweetened cranberries
½ cup celery, diced
⅓ cup pecans, chopped
¼ cup dried apricots, chopped
¾ cup mayonnaise
Salt and black pepper, to taste

INSTRUCTIONS

Combine chicken breast, apple, cranberries, celery, pecans, apricots, and mayonnaise. Stir to combine. Season with salt and black pepper.

Crab Salad with Cilantro

SERVES 3 `SNACK`

INGREDIENTS

- ¼ cup red onion, chopped
- 3 tbsps. fresh lime juice
- 2 tbsps. fresh cilantro, chopped
- 4 grape tomatoes, diced
- 1 tsp. olive oil
- ½ tsp. salt
- Black pepper, to taste
- 8 oz. imitation crab meat, chopped
- ½ cup celery, chopped
- 1 avocado, sliced

INSTRUCTIONS

Stir together red onion, lime juice, cilantro, grape tomatoes, olive oil, salt, and black pepper. Add imitation crabmeat and celery; toss gently and chill at least 1 hour. Top with sliced avocado.

For a sandwich option, spread some mashed avocado on croissants and add lettuce, alfalfa sprouts, and your crab salad.

Zesty Tuna Salad

SERVES 3-4 `SNACK`

INGREDIENTS

- 12.8 oz. light or white tuna
- ½ cup dill pickles, chopped
- 1 tbsp. dill pickle juice
- 1 tbsp. lemon juice
- ½ cup mayonnaise
- ½ cup pickled jalapeños, chopped
- 2 tbsps. red onion, minced
- 2 tbsps. scallions
- ½ tsp. yellow mustard
- ⅛ tsp. garlic powder
- ¼ cup carrot, shredded
- ½ poblano pepper, minced
- Salt and black pepper, to taste

INSTRUCTIONS

Mix tuna, dill pickles, pickle juice, lemon juice, mayo, pickled jalapeños, red onion, scallions, yellow mustard, garlic powder, carrot, and poblano pepper; season with salt and black pepper.

Ribeye, Spinach & Mashers

SERVES 4

INGREDIENTS

2 boneless ribeye steaks

Seasoned salt, to taste

Salt and black pepper, to taste

8 tbsps. butter

2½ lbs. russet potatoes

¾ cup half & half

8 oz. fresh mushrooms, thinly sliced

5 oz. fresh spinach

Vinaigrette of your choice, to taste

Garnishes: Crumbled blue cheese,
   French fried onions

INSTRUCTIONS

1 Season both sides of 2 boneless ribeye steaks with seasoned salt, salt, and black pepper. Melt 2 tbsps. butter in a skillet and cook steaks to desired doneness. Remove from skillet, let rest 15 minutes, then slice. Keep drippings in skillet.

2 Peel and quarter russet potatoes. Cook in salted boiling water until tender. Drain and return to the saucepan. Add 6 tbsps. butter, half & half, 1 tsp. salt, and a little black pepper; mash to desired consistency.

3 Meanwhile, sauté mushrooms using the drippings from the steak; season with salt and black pepper. Add spinach and a little vinaigrette; toss to coat.

4 Divide mashed potatoes, spinach-mushroom mixture, and steak among serving bowls.

5 Top with blue cheese and French fried onions.

6 Serve with additional vinaigrette.

Use up leftover mashed potatoes you've been saving in the fridge!

Sweet & Salty Chicken with Veg

SERVES 3

INGREDIENTS

1 spaghetti squash
3 tbsps. coconut oil
1 tbsp. maple syrup
¾ tsp. ground nutmeg
¾ tsp. cinnamon
¼ cup brown sugar
3 boneless chicken thighs

1 red onion
1 broccoli head
Coarse salt and black pepper,
   to taste
Sweet & Salty Chickpeas
   (see page 61)

INSTRUCTIONS

1 Preheat oven to 425°F. Cut 1 spaghetti squash in half lengthwise; remove seeds, poke a few holes in the flesh, and set on a parchment paper-lined baking pan, cut sides up. Rub 1 tbsp. coconut oil and 1 tbsp. maple syrup over cut sides and sprinkle with ground nutmeg and cinnamon.

2 Rub brown sugar evenly over 3 boneless chicken thighs; add to the baking pan.

3 Cut red onion into wedges and broccoli into large florets; toss with coconut oil and arrange on pan.

4 Sprinkle all the food liberally with coarse salt and black pepper. Roast for 30 minutes or until vegetables are tender and the chicken is done (165°F). Put under the broiler for a few minutes to brown further.

5 Use a fork to separate squash strands; add to serving bowls with chicken, onion, and broccoli. Serve with syrup and **Sweet & Salty Chickpeas**.

Sweet & Salty Chickpeas

`VEGAN` `SNACK`

INGREDIENTS

14-ounce can chickpeas
1 tsp. coarse salt
2 tsps. olive oil
1 tsp. cinnamon
1½ tsps. brown sugar

INSTRUCTIONS

1 Preheat the oven to 450°F and line a small, rimmed baking pan with parchment paper.

2 Drain and rinse the chickpeas and dump onto the pan in a single layer; sprinkle evenly with the salt. Bake for 40 minutes.

3 In a bowl, combine hot chickpeas with olive oil, cinnamon, and brown sugar. Stir until thoroughly combined.

Dill Pickle Burger Bowls

SERVES 4

INGREDIENTS

1 lb. ground beef

4 oz. mushrooms, sliced

½ tsp. onion powder

½ tsp. garlic powder

¼ tsp. paprika

Salt and black pepper, to taste

9-ounce package chopped salad kit with ranch dressing and croutons

1 cup cherry tomatoes, halved

1 avocado, sliced

1 small red onion, sliced

2 dill pickles, chopped

Garnishes: Dill weed, Parmesan cheese

INSTRUCTIONS

1 Cook ground beef until nearly done, crumbling it while it cooks. Add sliced mushrooms and cook until beef is done and mushrooms are tender; season with onion powder, garlic powder, paprika, salt, and black pepper.

2 Divide chopped salad kit, prepared ground beef, cherry tomatoes, avocado, red onion, and dill pickles among serving bowls.

3 Top with dill weed, Parmesan cheese, and the croutons from the salad kit. Serve with the dressing from the kit.

All-Green Salads

These meals are a veggie-lover's delight! Along with salad greens, these meals include a variety of scrumptious fruits and vegetables. While these recipes have been labeled with either "vegetarian" or "vegan," it's easy to customize these salads for your diet.

Chopped Veggie Bliss
with Basil Vinaigrette

SERVES 6 **VEGETARIAN**

SALAD

¼ to ½ lb. fresh asparagus

1 tbsp. olive oil

Salt, to taste

½ cup almonds, slivered

2 bell peppers, seeded & diced (any color)

3 celery ribs, sliced

2 medium carrots, chopped

1 cup small cauliflower florets

¼ cup red onion, chopped

½ cucumber, seeded & chopped

1 pt. grape or cherry tomatoes, halved (I used red & yellow)

½ to 1 poblano pepper, seeded & diced

1 cup white cheddar or mozzarella cheese, cubed

VINAIGRETTE

½ cup fresh basil, lightly packed

3 tbsps. lemon juice

1 tbsp. honey

Salt and black pepper, to taste

Scant ½ cup olive oil

INSTRUCTIONS

1 To make the **Basil Vinaigrette**, combine basil, lemon juice, honey, salt, and pepper in a food processor and pulse until basil is chopped. Slowly add the olive oil, processing until well blended.

2 For the salad, preheat the oven to 400°F and line a rimmed baking sheet with greased foil. Drizzle the asparagus with oil and season with salt; roast 5 to 7 minutes, turning once, until crisp-tender. Let cool, then cut into pieces.

3 While asparagus is cooking, toast the almonds in a dry skillet over medium heat, stirring until fragrant and lightly browned; set aside.

4 In a large bowl, combine the asparagus, bell peppers, celery, carrots, cauliflower, onion, cucumber, tomatoes, and poblano; sprinkle lightly with salt and toss gently. Let stand several minutes.

5 Add the cheese and toasted almonds. Drizzle the vinaigrette over the salad and toss well before serving.

Salad in a Jar
SERVES 1 VEGAN

Layer your favorite salad fixings in a quart-size mason jar, starting with 2 to 4 tbsp. dressing or salsa. Add sturdy veggies like bell peppers, onions, tomatoes, broccoli, carrots, and cucumbers next, followed by things like chickpeas, olives, and cooked pasta. Top with fresh greens, cheese, and nuts; cover tightly and refrigerate for up to 5 days.

Before eating, turn the jar upside down and shake well to mix the salad.

Autumn Fruit & Greens
with Sweet Poppy Seed Dressing

SERVES 6   VEGETARIAN

SALAD

1 large head romaine lettuce, torn
1 cup shredded Swiss cheese
1 cup salted cashews
¼ cup dried, sweetened cranberries
1 apple, cored & cubed
1 pear, cored & cubed

DRESSING

½ cup sugar
⅓ cup lemon juice
2 tsps. onion, finely chopped
1 tsp. dry mustard
½ tsp. salt
⅔ cup canola oil
1 tbsp. poppy seeds

INSTRUCTIONS

1   For the **Sweet Poppy Seed Dressing**, combine the sugar, lemon juice, onion, dry mustard, and salt in a blender and process until well mixed. Gradually blend in the canola oil until dressing is thick and smooth. Whisk in the poppy seeds and set aside.

2   In a large bowl, combine the lettuce, cheese, cashews, cranberries, apple, and pear; toss lightly.

3   Before serving, toss again with some of the dressing or serve it on the side.

Grilled Romaine & Veggies
with Balsamic-Herb Vinaigrette

SERVES 6 VEGAN

SALAD

12 asparagus spears, cut into
   1" pieces

2 cups grape or cherry tomatoes

2 cups white mushrooms, halved

1 orange bell pepper, cut into
   ½" pieces

½ green bell pepper, cut into
   ½" pieces

1½ tsps. olive oil

1 tsp. seasoned salt

1 tsp. onion powder

1 tsp. garlic powder

3 medium romaine hearts,
   halved lengthwise

Garnish: Shredded Romano cheese

VINAIGRETTE

¼ cup balsamic vinegar

2 tbsps. canola oil

1 tsp. dried basil

1 tsp. dried oregano

1 tsp. garlic powder

⅛ tsp. salt

For a different twist, toss these scrumptious grilled veggies over a bed of chilled greens and dress with the vinaigrette.

INSTRUCTIONS

1 Whisk together the **Balsamic-Herb Vinaigrette** ingredients and set aside to let flavors blend.

2 Toss the asparagus, tomatoes, mushrooms, and bell peppers into a big bowl with olive oil. Sprinkle with the seasoned salt, onion powder, and garlic powder and toss again until well coated.

3 Grill the asparagus mixture on an oiled grill pan over medium heat for 5 to 10 minutes or until browned and crisp-tender, turning occasionally; remove to a plate.

4 Brush the cut sides of romaine hearts with a little oil and grill them cut-side down for 3 to 4 minutes or until golden brown.

5 To serve, top the romaine with grilled asparagus mixture and a sprinkling of cheese. Drizzle with the vinaigrette and serve promptly.

Power Salad
with Sweet Onion Vinaigrette

SERVES 3 VEGAN

SALAD

- 3 cups mixed spring greens or baby kale
- 3 cups baby spinach
- 1 cup purple cabbage, shredded
- 2 carrots, julienned
- 1 cucumber, sliced
- ½ cup unsalted almonds, chopped
- 1 pt. fresh strawberries, sliced
- 1 pt. fresh blueberries
- 1 pt. red raspberries

VINAIGRETTE

- 1 tbsp. white balsamic vinegar
- 3 tbsps. olive oil
- 1 tbsp. sweet onion, minced
- Salt and black pepper, to taste

INSTRUCTIONS

1 In a large bowl, combine mixed spring greens, spinach, and cabbage. Divide among serving bowls. Top each serving with some raw carrots, cucumber, almonds, strawberries, blueberries, and raspberries.

2 To make the **Sweet Onion Vinaigrette**, whisk together white balsamic vinegar, olive oil, and sweet onion; season with salt and black pepper and mix well. Drizzle lightly over salads or serve the vinaigrette on the side.

Kale-Blueberry Combo
with Blueberry Dressing

SERVES 4 VEGETARIAN

SALAD

- 2 bunches kale
- ½ tsp. salt
- ¼ cup sweet corn kernels
- ¼ cup fresh blueberries
- ¼ cup cherry tomatoes, cut into wedges
- Garnishes: Sliced almonds, crumbled feta or goat cheese

DRESSING

- ⅔ cup fresh blueberries
- ¼ cup balsamic vinegar
- 2 tbsps. honey
- 2 tsps. Dijon mustard
- Salt and black pepper, to taste
- 6 tbsps. olive oil

INSTRUCTIONS

1 Remove stems from kale and tear leaves into a bowl. Sprinkle with salt and massage with fingers until kale is dark green and tender. Divide kale among serving bowls and top with sweet corn kernels, blueberries, and cherry tomato wedges. Sprinkle with almonds and cheese.

2 To make the **Blueberry Dressing**, combine blueberries, balsamic vinegar, honey, mustard, salt, and black pepper in a food processor or blender. Process to chop the berries, then slowly add olive oil and continue to blend until thickened. Serve the dressing alongside the salad.

Sweet & Crunchy Sprouts Slaw
with Maple-Balsamic Vinaigrette

SERVES 4 VEGETARIAN

SALAD

½ cup pine nuts

12 oz. fresh Brussels sprouts

¼ cup cashews or pecans, chopped

¼ cup dried, sweetened cherries

⅓ cup gorgonzola, crumbled, or
   Swiss cheese, cubed

1 pear, seeded & sliced

½ cup French fried onions

VINAIGRETTE

2 tbsps. olive oil

2 tbsps. white balsamic vinegar

1½ tbsps. pure maple syrup

½ tsp. Dijon mustard

Salt and black pepper, to taste

INSTRUCTIONS

1 Combine the **Maple-Balsamic Vinaigrette** ingredients in a jar with
  tight-fitting lid; cover and shake well. Set aside.

2 In a small dry skillet over medium-high heat, toast the pine nuts, tossing
  often, until golden brown and fragrant; let cool.

3 Remove the outer leaves of sprouts and thinly shred each one,
  discarding the cores.

4 In a large bowl, toss the shredded sprouts with some of the
  prepared vinaigrette.

5 Add the cashews, cherries, cheese, and pear, then toss lightly. Top with
  onions and cooled pine nuts and serve with the remaining vinaigrette.

Green Bean-Basil Combo
with Balsamic Vinaigrette

SERVES 2 **VEGETARIAN**

SALAD

¾ lb. fresh green beans

4 cups leaf lettuce, torn

½ pt. grape tomatoes, halved

¼ cup fresh basil, shredded

2 tbsps. pistachios, shelled, salted & roasted

3 oz. feta cheese, crumbled

VINAIGRETTE

½ shallot, minced

1½ tbsps. balsamic vinegar

2 tbsps. olive oil

Salt and black pepper, to taste

INSTRUCTIONS

1 Trim and halve green beans and cook in boiling water for 3 minutes; transfer to ice water to cool for 2 minutes. Drain and pat dry.

2 To make the **Balsamic Vinaigrette**, combine shallot, balsamic vinegar, and olive oil in a jar with a tight-fitting lid; cover and shake until well blended. Season with salt and black pepper and shake again.

3 Spread lettuce on a platter and top with the green beans, tomatoes, and basil. Before serving, drizzle with the vinaigrette and sprinkle with pistachios and feta cheese.

Grilled Corn & Jicama Salad

SERVES 8 VEGAN

INGREDIENTS

1 jicama (about 1 ½ lbs.)

1 bottle Italian dressing

2 tbsps. yellow mustard

4 ears fresh sweet corn

½ lb. fresh asparagus, trimmed
& halved

2 tomatoes, diced

½ cup fresh basil, chopped

INSTRUCTIONS

1 Peel and cube jicama and toss into a large bowl with ½ cup Italian dressing; set aside.

2 Mix yellow mustard and 2 tbsps. Italian dressing in a bowl; coat sweet corn with mustard mixture. Grill the corn over medium heat for 15 to 20 minutes or until tender, turning frequently and brushing with any remaining mixture. Let cool.

3 Meanwhile, cook asparagus in boiling water for 2 to 4 minutes, just until crisp-tender; drain and rinse in cold water.

4 Slice corn off the cob and toss into the bowl with jicama. Add the asparagus, tomatoes, and basil; toss lightly. Chill or serve right away.

Huevos Rancheros Salad
with Salsa-Style Dressing

SERVES 6 **VEGETARIAN**

SALAD

- 6 corn tortillas
- ¼ cup olive oil, divided
- Coarse salt, to taste
- 12 cups mixed spring greens or arugula
- 6 eggs
- Salt and black pepper, to taste
- ½ cup queso fresco (Mexican cheese), crumbled

DRESSING

- 15-ounce can black beans, drained & rinsed
- 3 plum tomatoes, chopped
- ½ red onion, chopped
- ½ cup olive oil
- ½ cup lime juice
- 3 tbsps. fresh cilantro, roughly chopped
- ¾ tsp. hot sauce
- ¾ tsp. salt

INSTRUCTIONS

1 Combine the **Salsa-Style Dressing** ingredients in a medium bowl; stir well and set aside.

2 To prep the tortillas for the salad, use 1 tbsp. olive oil to brush both sides of all tortillas and sprinkle them lightly with coarse salt. Toast the tortillas under a broiler until lightly browned, 1 to 2 minutes per side. Cut into wedges and let cool.

3 Set aside ½ cup of the prepped dressing; divide the greens among serving bowls and top evenly with the remaining dressing.

4 In a nonstick skillet, heat the remaining 3 tbsps. olive oil over medium heat and fry the eggs about 3 minutes, seasoning with salt and pepper. Lightly spoon some of the oil over the tops of eggs or add a little water to the skillet and cover tightly until whites are opaque and yolks are cooked to desired doneness.

5 Transfer one egg onto each salad, sprinkle with cheese, and top with the reserved salsa dressing. Serve immediately with tortilla wedges.

Western Dressing

INGREDIENTS

⅔ cup ketchup
⅓ cup olive oil
⅓ cup apple cider vinegar
⅓ cup sugar
1 tbsp. honey
½ tsp. Worcestershire sauce
¼ tsp. onion powder
¼ tsp. garlic powder
¼ tsp. salt

INSTRUCTIONS

In a bowl, whisk together ketchup, olive oil, apple cider vinegar, and sugar. Add the rest of the ingredients; whisk again. Store in the refrigerator.

Egg Salad
with Kale Pesto

SERVES 4 `VEGETARIAN` `SNACK`

SALAD

8 eggs, hard-boiled
¼ cup plain Greek yogurt
¼ cup mayonnaise
Salt and black pepper, to taste

SAUCE

1½ cups kale leaves
2 garlic cloves
3 tbsps. pine nuts
¼ cup Parmesan
   cheese, grated
Salt and black pepper, to taste
⅓ cup olive oil

INSTRUCTIONS

1 For the **Kale Pesto Sauce**, toss kale leaves, garlic cloves, pine nuts, and Parmesan cheese into a food processor; season with salt and black pepper. Pulse until chopped, then slowly add olive oil, processing until well blended.

2 Roughly mash eggs. Stir in Greek yogurt and mayonnaise, plus salt and black pepper.

For a sandwich, spread pesto on thin buns and add lettuce, tomatoes, and egg salad.

Pasta
& Noodles

Everything from classic pasta salad to a
hearty ramen bowl can be found in this
section. There is such a variety of pasta and
noodles, that every meal tastes unique.

Broccoli & Chickpea Pasta Salad
with Creamy Oregano Dressing

SERVES 6

SALAD

- 3 cups uncooked pasta
- 2 cups fresh broccoli, chopped
- 1¾ cups grape tomatoes, halved
- 15-ounce can chickpeas, drained & rinsed
- ½ cup feta cheese, crumbled
- Black pepper, to taste

DRESSING

- ¾ tsp. garlic, minced
- ¼ tsp. salt
- ¾ cup buttermilk
- 6 tbsps. mayonnaise
- ¼ cup fresh oregano, chopped (or 1½ tbsps. dried)
- 1½ tbsps. white wine vinegar

INSTRUCTIONS

1 Prepare the **Creamy Oregano Dressing** in a small bowl by mashing the garlic and salt together with the back of a spoon. Add the remaining dressing ingredients and whisk well; set aside.

2 Meanwhile, cook the pasta in lightly salted boiling water according to package directions. Drain and rinse in cold water; transfer to a large bowl.

3 Add the broccoli, tomatoes, chickpeas, and cheese to the bowl of pasta. Season with pepper and toss everything with enough of the prepared dressing to coat well. Cover and chill for 1 hour before serving.

Italian Pasta Bowl
with Italian Vinaigrette

SERVES 6

SALAD

- 2½ cups uncooked medium pasta
- 1½ cups fennel bulb, chopped
- ½ cup red bell pepper, diced
- ½ cup green bell pepper, diced
- 1 cup canned chopped artichoke hearts, drained
- 1 cup cannellini beans, drained & rinsed
- 1 cup salami, chopped
- 1 cup grape tomatoes, halved
- 3 tbsps. pepperoncini, chopped
- Black pepper, to taste
- ⅓ cup shredded provolone or Monterey Jack cheese (optional)

VINAIGRETTE

- ¼ cup olive oil
- ¼ cup chicken broth
- ¼ cup red wine vinegar
- 1 tbsp. Italian seasoning
- 2 tbsps. shallots, minced
- ¼ tsp. garlic salt
- ¼ tsp. salt
- ¼ tsp. black pepper

I used elbow pasta, but you can change it up with spirals, shells, or another fun shape.

INSTRUCTIONS

1 Combine the **Italian Vinaigrette** ingredients in a shaker jar; cover and shake like crazy. Reserve for later use.

2 Cook the pasta in lightly salted boiling water according to package directions. Drain, rinse in cold water, and transfer to a large bowl.

3 To put the salad together, add the fennel, bell peppers, artichokes, beans, salami, tomatoes, and pepperoncini to the bowl of pasta; season with black pepper. Add the reserved vinaigrette and toss until well coated.

4 Cover and chill at least 1 hour. Sprinkle with cheese before serving, if you'd like.

Try substituting chunks of fresh honeydew melon for the cantaloupe in this salad.

Cantaloupe & Chicken Bowties
with Creamy Tarragon Dressing

SERVES 6

SALAD

3 cups bowtie pasta

2 cups cantaloupe, cubed

2 cups cooked chicken, cubed

3-ounce pkg. prosciutto, chopped

2 cups fresh spinach

¼ cup dried, sweetened cranberries

Black pepper, to taste

DRESSING

½ tsp. garlic, minced

¼ tsp. salt

½ cup buttermilk

¼ cup mayonnaise

3 tbsps. fresh tarragon, chopped
(or 1 tbsp. dried)

1 tbsp. white vinegar

½ tsp. sugar

INSTRUCTIONS

1 To make the **Creamy Tarragon Dressing**, mash the garlic and salt together in a small bowl. Add the remaining dressing ingredients and whisk until well blended. Refrigerate until needed.

2 Cook the pasta in lightly salted boiling water according to package directions; drain and rinse in cold water.

3 Add the cantaloupe, chicken, and prosciutto to the bowl of pasta. Pour the dressing over the salad and toss well. Chill for up to 1 hour before serving, if you'd like.

4 To assemble the salad, arrange some spinach on each serving bowl and spoon some of the pasta mixture on top. Sprinkle with cranberries and season with pepper.

Sweet & Sour Dressing

INGREDIENTS

6 tbsps. sugar

6 tbsps. white vinegar

¼ cup canola oil

2 tsps. creamy horseradish

½ tsp. dry mustard

1 tsp. salt

¼ to ½ tsp. black pepper

INSTRUCTIONS

In a shaker jar, combine the ingredients; cover and shake well. Store in the refrigerator.

Spicy Shrimp & Ramen Noodles
with Avocado Coconut-Lime Dressing

SERVES 4

MEAL

- 1 lb. shrimp, thawed, peeled & deveined
- ½ lime juice
- 1 tsp. Creole seasoning
- ½ tsp. smoked paprika
- Pinch of sea salt
- (3) 3-ounce pkgs. ramen noodles
- 1 pt. cherry tomatoes, sliced
- 1 to 2 scallions, sliced
- ¼ cup bacon bits
- 1 jalapeño pepper, sliced

DRESSING

- 1 avocado, peeled & pitted
- ⅔ cup coconut milk
- ½ lime juice
- ½ lemon juice
- 1 tsp. garlic, minced
- ½ jalapeño, minced
- 1 tbsp. cilantro

Garnishes like fresh cilantro and dill, while adding some flavor, are mostly added to make bowls extra pretty. Include them if you'd like or leave them off.

INSTRUCTIONS

1 To make the **Avocado Coconut-Lime Dressing**, combine ingredients in a food processor or blender. Process until smooth, adding a little more coconut milk if needed to make it pourable. Season to taste and process again. Set aside.

2 Toss shrimp with a little olive oil and lime juice. Sprinkle with Creole seasoning, smoked paprika, and sea salt; toss to combine. Cook in a little hot olive oil until pink and opaque; set aside.

3 Prepare ramen noodles according to package directions; drain and cool for a few minutes. Discard seasoning packets or save for a different use. Stir ¾ of the dressing into the noodles.

4 Arrange noodles and shrimp in bowls. Top with tomatoes, scallions, bacon bits, and jalapeño. Serve with the remaining dressing.

Salmon Noodle Bowls
with Sriracha-Honey Vinaigrette

SERVES 4

MEAL

(4) 4 oz. salmon fillets

Sea salt and black pepper, to taste

Hoisin sauce, to taste

2 tbsps. apple cider vinegar

1 tbsp. honey

½ head red cabbage

2 tbsps. rice vinegar

2 tsps. sesame oil

1 tsp. sugar

1 seedless cucumber

(2) 14-ounce pkg. rice noodles
   (enough for 4 servings)

Garnishes: Smoked
   almonds, scallions

VINAIGRETTE

2 tbsps. apple cider vinegar

2 tbsps. olive oil

1 tbsp. Sriracha sauce

1 tsp. honey

¼ tsp. sea salt

INSTRUCTIONS

1 Preheat the broiler. Remove skin from salmon fillets and season with sea salt and black pepper. Coat each fillet with hoisin sauce and arrange on a greased rimmed baking pan. Broil for a few minutes on each side, until opaque throughout.

2 In a big bowl, whisk together apple cider vinegar, honey, and ¼ tsp. each sea salt and black pepper. Shred red cabbage and add to the vinegar mixture; toss to coat. Set aside at least 10 minutes, stirring occasionally.

3 In a separate bowl, whisk together rice vinegar, sesame oil, sugar, and a pinch of sea salt. Thinly slice cucumber and add to the bowl. Toss to combine and set aside at least 10 minutes, stirring occasionally.

4 Cook rice noodles according to package directions to make 4 servings.

5 To make **Sriracha-Honey Vinaigrette**, whisk together ingredients.

6 Divide noodles and cabbage among serving bowls. Top each with prepped cucumber slices, a salmon fillet, almonds, and scallions. Serve with vinaigrette.

This recipe, like many others in this book, is great for grab-and-go meals.

Asparagus, Pork & Pasta

SERVES 2

INGREDIENTS

4 bacon strips

8 oz. pork loin

Smoked paprika, to taste

½ large yellow onion

⅓ cup dry white wine

2 tsps. garlic, minced

1 cup tomatoes, diced

3 cups chicken broth

4 oz. noodles (I used Mafalda)

6 oz. asparagus, cut into 1" pieces

Garlic powder, to taste

Salt and black pepper, to taste

Garnish: Scallions

INSTRUCTIONS

1 Dice bacon strips and cook in a big, deep saucepan until crisp; drain on paper towels, reserving drippings in pan.

2 Cut pork loin into thin strips; sprinkle with smoked paprika and cook in reserved bacon drippings until golden brown and cooked through. Remove from skillet and cover to keep warm.

3 Chop onion and add to hot drippings in skillet. Cook for 3 minutes, stirring often. Add white wine and garlic; bring to a boil. Reduce heat and simmer for 5 minutes, stirring to scrape up browned bits.

4 Add tomatoes to the skillet with the onion; bring to a boil. Reduce heat, simmer uncovered for 5 minutes, stirring occasionally. Stir in chicken broth and ½ tsp. smoked paprika; bring to a boil. Stir in noodles; bring to a boil and cook until tender, stirring occasionally, adding asparagus during the last 2 minutes of cooking time.

5 Divide pasta mixture among serving bowls; season with garlic powder, salt, and black pepper. Add pork and top with bacon, scallions, and additional diced tomato.

Cabbage, Eggs & Lo Mein

SERVES 2 **VEGETARIAN**

INGREDIENTS

Quick-Pickled Carrots (see page 93)

1 small green cabbage

2 tbsps. soy sauce

½ tsp. sesame seeds

4-ounce pkg. lo mein noodles

2 eggs

1 tbsp. olive oil

Salt and white pepper, to taste

Garnishes: Sesame seeds, scallions, red pepper flakes

INSTRUCTIONS

1 Make the **Quick-Pickled Carrots**.

2 Heat the broiler. Remove the core from cabbage and cut into ¼" thick slices; brush olive oil over both sides and broil for a couple of minutes, until tender and lightly charred.

3 Measure out 3 tbsps. of the liquid from the Quick-Pickled Carrots and mix with soy sauce and sesame seeds. Set aside for serving.

4 Cook lo mein noodles according to package directions.

5 Cook eggs sunny-side-up in 1 tbsp. olive oil, spooning some of the hot oil over the top to help the whites set; season with salt and white pepper.

6 Divide the noodles, cabbage, and Quick-Pickled Carrots among serving bowls. Top with eggs.

7 Sprinkle with sesame seed, scallions, and red pepper flakes. Serve with the prepared soy sauce mixture.

Quick-Pickled Carrots

`VEGAN`   `SNACK`

INGREDIENTS

½ cup carrots, thinly sliced
1½ tsps. rice vinegar
1½ tsps. white vinegar, distilled
1 tsp. honey
¼ tsp. sea salt

INSTRUCTIONS

Put carrots into a heat-safe jar. In a small saucepan, combine rice vinegar, white vinegar, 3 tbsp. water, honey, and sea salt; bring to a boil then pour over the carrots in the jar. Let stand at least an hour. The longer they set, the more flavor they'll have.

Keep 3 tbsps. of liquids for **Cabbage, Eggs, & Lo Mein** recipe.

Citrus Salmon & Pasta
with Citrus Marinade

SERVES 3

MEAL

3 salmon fillets

6 pineapple slices

1 pkg. pasta (enough for 3 servings)

⅓ cup butter

½ tsp. sea salt

1 tsp. garlic powder

1 lime juice

15-ounce can black beans, drained & rinsed

1 avocado, cubed

1 large tomato, sliced

1 jalapeño pepper, sliced

Garnishes: Orange zest, lime zest

MARINADE

1 orange

1 lime

½ cup orange juice

1 to 2 tbsps. lime juice

½ tsp. ground cumin

½ tsp. ground oregano

¼ tsp. sea salt

⅛ tsp. black pepper

2 tbsps. chopped fresh cilantro

1 tsp. minced garlic

¼ cup olive oil

INSTRUCTIONS

1 To make the **Citrus Marinade**, zest orange and lime; set the zest aside to use for bowls. Whisk together the rest of the ingredients.

2 Set aside ¼ cup of marinade and pour the remainder into a zippered plastic bag; add 3 salmon fillets to the bag and marinate for 10 minutes.

3 Preheat oven to 425°F. Arrange the salmon on a baking pan and drizzle with olive oil. Bake for 10 to 12 minutes until done. Discard marinade from bag.

4 Meanwhile, preheat a grill pan over medium-high heat. Brush vegetable oil over both sides of pineapple slices and grill for 10 minutes or until grill marks appear, flipping halfway through. Brush the set-aside Citrus Marinade over the pineapple during the last few minutes of cooking time. Cut pineapple into chunks.

5 Cook pasta according to package directions to make 3 servings; drain and return to pan. Melt butter; stir in sea salt and garlic powder, then stir into the pasta. Squeeze in lime juice.

6 Divide black beans and pasta among serving bowls. Add the salmon, pineapple, avocado, and tomato. Squeeze lime juice over the top.

7 Top with jalapeño slices; add orange zest and lime zest set aside from making the Citrus Marinade.

Tortellini, Bacon & Broccoli

SERVES 4

INGREDIENTS

9-ounce pkg. three-cheese tortellini

½ lb. bacon strips

2 cups fresh broccoli, chopped

½ pt. grape tomatoes, halved

1 to 2 scallions, sliced

½ cup bottled coleslaw dressing

INSTRUCTIONS

1 Cook tortellini in boiling water according to package directions; drain, rinse with cold water, and chill about 30 minutes.

2 Cook bacon strips in a large skillet over medium heat until almost crisp. Drain on paper towels and when cool, crumble the bacon; discard the drippings.

3 Combine the tortellini, bacon, broccoli, tomatoes, and scallions in a large salad bowl and toss with coleslaw dressing until evenly coated. Cover and chill before serving.

Grain Bowls

There are a ton of grains out there that are both delicious and nutritious! By including fresh flavors and unique dressings, each meal is completely different from the last while keeping your cooking time down.

Sweet Potato & Farro
with Dijon Vinaigrette

SERVES 2   VEGAN

MEAL

1 sweet potato

¼ cup almonds, sliced

1 pkg. farro (enough for 2 servings)

1 carrot

3 to 4 radishes

2 cups mixed salad greens

1 apple, sliced

VINAIGRETTE

⅓ cup olive oil

¼ cup lemon juice

1 tsp. Dijon mustard

½ tsp. honey

1 garlic clove, minced

Salt and black pepper, to taste

INSTRUCTIONS

1   Preheat oven to 400°F. Cube sweet potato; drizzle with olive oil, sprinkle with salt and black pepper, and roast for 25 to 30 minutes or until crisp-tender.

2   Reduce oven temp to 350°F. Toss almonds into a small baking pan and bake 8 to 10 minutes, until golden brown, shaking the pan occasionally. Set sweet potatoes and almonds aside.

3   Cook farro according to package directions to make 2 servings; cool slightly.

4   To prepare the **Dijon Vinaigrette**, whisk together ingredients.

5   Using a vegetable peeler, shave carrot into ribbons; slice radishes. Arrange in bowls with greens, farro, sweet potato, and apple slices. Top with almonds. Serve with vinaigrette.

Coconut Chicken & Quinoa

SERVES 1

INGREDIENTS

1 pkg. quinoa

4 oz. chicken breast

14-ounce can coconut milk

Sea salt and black pepper, to taste

1 cup kale leaves

1 lemon

¼ cup bean sprouts

1 cucumber, sliced

1 shallot, sliced

1 avocado, sliced

Garnish: Sesame seeds

1 bottle apple cider vinaigrette

INSTRUCTIONS

1 Cook quinoa according to package directions to make 1 serving.

2 Put chicken breast into a small saucepan. Add coconut milk and enough water to cover chicken by 1"; bring to a simmer, cover the saucepan, and turn off the heat. Let set 30 to 40 minutes to poach (chicken is done at 165°F). Drain the milk, slice the chicken, and season with sea salt and black pepper.

3 Tear a couple of kale leaves into bite-size pieces and rub with a little lemon juice to soften; put into a serving bowl with the quinoa, chicken, bean sprouts, cucumber, shallot, and avocado. Season with sea salt and black pepper. Top with sesame seeds and lemon wedges for squeezing.

4 Serve with apple cider vinaigrette.

Kale Chips

VEGETARIAN　**SNACK**

INGREDIENTS

1 medium-sized bunch kale

2 tsps. olive oil

Sea salt, to taste

Garlic powder, to taste

Grated Parmesan cheese, to taste (optional)

These make a crunchy addition to any bowl and are delicious on their own anytime. Also a great way to use up your extra kale!

INSTRUCTIONS

1　Preheat the oven to 300°F.

2　Wash and thoroughly dry the kale. Remove the big center stems and tear the leaves into chip-sized pieces. Toss pieces onto a big, rimmed baking pan.

3　Drizzle olive oil evenly over the kale and massage into the leaves, making sure they're thoroughly coated. Arrange leaves in a single layer then sprinkle with sea salt and garlic powder.

4　Bake for 10 minutes, rotate the pan, and flip any chips that might be getting crisp. Bake for an additional 7 to 15 minutes, checking every couple of minutes to prevent overbrowning.

5　Remove the pan from the oven and let the chips set on the pan for a few minutes to finish crisping.

Mediterranean Chicken & Couscous
with Buttermilk Dressing

SERVES 4

MEAL

1 tbsp. olive oil

10-ounce pkg. couscous

2¼ cups water

3 cup rotisserie chicken, shredded

1 cucumber, sliced

1 red onion, sliced

1 pt. cherry tomatoes, halved

1 cup feta cheese

Fresh dill, to taste

DRESSING

½ cup full-fat plain Greek yogurt

3 tbsps. full-fat buttermilk

1½ tbsps. white vinegar, distilled

½ tsp. salt

½ tsp. black pepper

1 garlic clove, minced

1 tbsp. fresh dill, chopped

INSTRUCTIONS

1 Heat olive oil in a big saucepan over medium-high heat. Add couscous; heat for 3 minutes, until lightly toasted, stirring often. Add water; bring to a boil. Reduce heat, cover, and simmer 14 minutes or until tender. Drain, rinse with cold water, and divide among serving bowls.

2 Make **Buttermilk Dressing** by whisking together Greek yogurt, buttermilk, white vinegar, salt, black pepper, and garlic until well blended. Stir in dill.

3 Divide chicken among the bowls along with cucumber, red onion, and cherry tomatoes.

4 Top with feta cheese and dill. Serve with dressing.

Green Goddess & Farro
with Green Goddess Dressing

SERVES 4 `VEGETARIAN`

MEAL

- 1⅓ cups farro (or enough for 4 servings)
- 1-ounce pkg. dry onion soup mix
- 6 cups broccoli florets
- 2 tbsps. olive oil
- ½ tsp. salt
- ¼ tsp. black pepper
- 4 eggs
- 8 oz. sugar snap peas
- 2 tomatoes, cut into wedges

DRESSING

- 2 cups plain Greek yogurt
- 2 tbsps. lemon juice
- 2 tbsps. olive oil
- 2 garlic cloves
- ¼ tsp. sea salt
- Pinch of black pepper
- ⅓ cup chives, chopped
- ⅓ cup fresh basil, packed
- ¼ cup fresh mint

INSTRUCTIONS

1 To make **Green Goddess Dressing**, combine Greek yogurt, lemon juice, olive oil, garlic cloves, sea salt, and black pepper in a food processor; purée until smooth. Add chives, basil, and mint; pulse until combined.

2 Cook farro according to package directions to make 4 servings, adding half of dry onion soup mix to the water.

3 Preheat oven to 375°F. Toss broccoli florets with olive oil, salt, and black pepper on a rimmed baking pan. Roast 12 to 15 minutes, until lightly browned and crisp-tender.

4 Bring a medium pot of water to a boil. Add eggs, cover, and cook 7 minutes. Transfer to a bowl of ice water; once eggs are cool to the touch, peel and halve them.

5 Add sugar snap peas to boiling water; cook 1 to 2 minutes, until bright green, then transfer to ice water.

6 Divide farro, broccoli, and snap peas among serving bowls. Top with eggs and tomato wedges. Serve with dressing.

Mid-East Chicken & Quinoa
with Tahini Sauce

SERVES 2

MEAL

Homemade Pita Chips (see page 108)

1 cup cucumber

1 cup cherry tomatoes

¼ small red onion

½ red bell pepper

½ green bell pepper

1 lemon

2 boneless chicken breast halves

2 tbsps. olive oil

1 garlic clove, minced

1 tsp. ground cumin

½ tsp. smoked paprika

¼ tsp. ground turmeric

⅛ tsp. cayenne pepper

1 cup quinoa

1½ cups water

Salt and black pepper, to taste

SAUCE

¼ cup tahini

1 clove garlic, minced

½ lemon juice

3 tbsps. warm water

⅛ tsp. salt

⅛ tsp. black pepper

⅛ tsp. paprika

INSTRUCTIONS

1   Make the **Tahini Sauce** by whisking together tahini, garlic, and lemon juice. Slowly whisk in warm water until smooth. Stir in salt, black pepper, and paprika.

2   Make **Homemade Pita Chips**. Dice cucumber and halve cherry tomatoes. Set aside.

3   Chop onion and bell peppers; toss into a small bowl. Juice lemon; stir half into the vegetables and set the remaining juice aside.

4   Using paper towels, pat dry chicken breast halves; pound ¼" thick. In a zippered plastic bag, combine the set-aside lemon juice, 1 tbsp. olive oil, garlic, ground cumin, smoked paprika, ground turmeric, and cayenne pepper. Add chicken, turn to coat, and marinate for 15 minutes.

5   Meanwhile, toast quinoa in a medium saucepan until light golden, stirring constantly. Add water and bring to a boil; reduce heat to low and cook partially covered for 13 minutes until all liquid is absorbed. Fluff with a fork; season with salt and black pepper.

6   Heat 1 tbsp. olive oil in a big skillet; add the chicken (discard marinade) and cook until done (165°F), flipping once. Transfer to a cutting board; let rest 5 minutes, then slice.

7   Divide quinoa among serving bowls. Add chicken and set-aside cucumber, tomatoes, and pepper mixture. Serve with sauce and pita chips.

Homemade Pita Chips

VEGAN   **SNACK**

INGREDIENTS

Pita bread rounds (as many as desired)

Olive oil, to taste

Za'atar or salt and black pepper, to taste

INSTRUCTIONS

1 Preheat the oven to 425°F. Split pita breads by cutting through the center to make two flat rounds (if your pita breads don't have a pocket but are thick flat rounds, don't split them).

2 Brush both sides of each round with olive oil and sprinkle with Za'atar or salt and black pepper. Cut each round into eight triangles. Arrange in a single layer on a rimmed baking pan.

3 Bake each side for 5 minutes or until golden brown and crisp.

Cumin Hummus

VEGAN **SNACK**

INGREDIENTS

- 14-ounce can chickpeas
- ¼ cup tahini
- ¼ cup lemon juice
- 2 tbsps. olive oil
- 1 garlic clove, minced
- ½ tsp. ground cumin
- ½ tsp. salt
- 2 tbsps. water
- Paprika, to taste

Making your own pita chips is rewarding and utterly yummy. Mix and match with your favorite meal!

INSTRUCTIONS

1 Drain and rinse the chickpeas.

2 In a food processor, combine the tahini and lemon juice; process for 1½ minutes, scraping the sides once. Add olive oil, garlic, cumin, and salt; process until well blended. Add the chickpeas and process for 1 minute; scrape the bowl and process again until thick and smooth. With the food processor running, slowly add water through the chute, until very smooth. Salt to taste.

3 Transfer to a serving bowl, drizzle with olive oil, and sprinkle with paprika.

Hawaiian Ham & Couscous

SERVES 2

INGREDIENTS

1 pkg. couscous
(enough for 2 servings)

¾ cup chicken stock

2 red bell peppers

½ lb. ham, fully cooked

1 cup pineapple chunks

1 tbsp. vegetable oil

2 tbsp. brown sugar

1 tbsp. water

½ tsp. salt

1 tsp. black pepper

Garnishes: Cilantro, mint,
macadamia nuts

INSTRUCTIONS

1 Cook couscous according to package directions to make 2
servings, using chicken stock for the cooking liquid.

2 Meanwhile, cut bell peppers and ham into bite-size pieces.

3 Heat vegetable oil in a big skillet over medium heat
and add the bell peppers, cooking until lightly charred,
flipping occasionally.

4 Stir in the ham, pineapple, brown sugar, water, salt, and
black pepper. Increase heat to high and cook to lightly char.
Reduce heat to medium-low, stir, and simmer for 5 minutes.

5 Divide couscous among serving bowls and add ham mixture,
cilantro, mint, and nuts.

Beet & Shrimp Barley Bowls
with White Wine Vinaigrette

SERVES 2–4

MEAL

- 15-ounce can whole beets, drained
- 5-ounce bag mixed spring greens
- 1 cup zucchini, sliced
- 1 cup fennel bulb, thinly sliced
- 1 cup barley, cooked & cooled
- 4 to 8 oz. shrimp, cooked & peeled (I used thawed salad shrimp)

VINAIGRETTE

- ¼ cup olive oil
- 2 tbsps. white wine vinegar
- 1 tsp. Dijon mustard
- 1 tsp. shallot, minced
- ½ tsp. black pepper

INSTRUCTIONS

1 Slice beets into wedges; pat dry. In a big bowl, combine mixed spring greens, zucchini, fennel bulb, barley, prepared beet wedges, and shrimp.

2 To make the **White Wine Vinaigrette**, whisk together ingredients until well blended. Drizzle over the salad and toss lightly just before serving.

BBQ Pork & Polenta

SERVES 4

INGREDIENTS

1 ¼ to 1 ½ lb. pork loin

1 ½ cup barbeque sauce

1 pkg. polenta (enough for 4 servings)

¼ cup mascarpone cheese

1 tbsp. butter

½ tsp. salt

2 cups pineapple chunks (or tidbits)

1 cup guacamole

Lime juice, to taste

Garnish: Fresh cilantro

INSTRUCTIONS

1   Place pork loin into a slow cooker and add BBQ sauce. Cover and cook on high 4 to 6 hours, until the meat falls apart easily. Shred the meat and keep warm.

2   Prepare polenta according to package directions to make 4 servings. Once thickened and most of the water is absorbed, remove from the heat. Stir in mascarpone cheese, butter, and salt. Divide among serving bowls.

3   Top bowls with pork, pineapple, and guacamole. Squeeze lime juice over each. Garnish with cilantro.

Polenta sets up once it cools, so for creamy, warm goodness, put bowls together right before you sit down to eat.

Italian Meatballs & Quinoa
with Spicy Lemon Vinaigrette

SERVES 4

INGREDIENTS

1 pkg. tri-colored quinoa (enough for 4 servings)

1 pkg. meatballs (enough for 12 to 16, or as many as desired)

3 Roma tomatoes

1 fennel bulb

1 to 2 cups olives

2 pepperoncini, thinly sliced

Garnish: Feta cheese

VINAIGRETTE

¼ cup olive oil

1 lemon juice

1½ tbsps. white wine vinegar

¼ to ½ tsp. red pepper flakes

Salt and black pepper, to taste

INSTRUCTIONS

1 To make the **Spicy Lemon Vinaigrette**, whisk together ingredients in a bowl. Refrigerate until needed.

2 Cook tri-colored quinoa according to package directions to make 4 servings.

3 While quinoa is cooking, preheat the oven according to meatball package directions. Bake meatballs.

4 Slice tomatoes and shave fennel bulb.*

5 Divide the quinoa, meatballs, tomatoes, and fennel among serving bowls. Top with olives, pepperoncini, and feta cheese. Serve with vinaigrette.

*Or roast the veggies by cutting the tomatoes into wedges and thinly slicing the fennel; drizzle with olive oil and sprinkle with salt and black pepper. Bake the fennel on a rimmed baking pan at 475°F for 20 minutes. Add the tomatoes to the pan with the fennel and bake for an additional 7 to 10 minutes.

Pesto, Greens & Grains
with Creamy Pesto Sauce

SERVES 2 VEGETARIAN

MEAL

1 cup shelled
  edamame, thawed

8.5-ounce pkg. heat & serve
  7-grain medley

2 cups mixed salad greens

½ yellow bell pepper

2 radishes

1 jalapeño pepper

Garnishes: Corn nuts,
  fresh parsley

SAUCE

½ cup fresh basil, packed

1 garlic clove, roughly chopped

3 tbsps. pine nuts

½ cup olive oil

2 tbsps. fresh lemon juice

¼ tsp. salt

¼ tsp. black pepper

3 tbsps. sour cream

1½ tbsps. mayonnaise

INSTRUCTIONS

1 Heat a nonstick skillet over high heat. Add edamame and heat until lightly browned, shaking
  the skillet occasionally; set aside to cool.

2 Heat grain medley according to package directions; set aside to cool.

3 To make the **Creamy Pesto Sauce**, combine basil, garlic, and pine nuts in a food processor.
  With the processor running, drizzle in olive oil, lemon juice, salt, and black pepper. Stir in sour
  cream and mayo.

4 Divide the grains and salad greens among serving bowls; season with salt.

5 Cut bell pepper into chunks and slice radishes and jalapeño; add to bowls. Toss on some corn
  nuts and parsley. Serve with sauce.

Rice Bowls

Rice is a beloved staple across so many cultures that these recipes include a ton of flavors and culinary inspirations. Cauliflower rice is also included in this category for another healthy option. With these recipes, you can travel the world, eat hearty or light, and enjoy something delicious no matter what you choose!

Veggies & Brown Rice
with Whole Lemon Dressing

SERVES 4 VEGAN

MEAL

- 1 pkg. brown rice (enough for 4 servings)
- 2 tbsps. sesame seeds
- ½ head cabbage
- 1 cup sugar snap peas
- 2 tbsps. cilantro, chopped
- 3 carrots
- 15-ounce can black beans, drained & rinsed
- 4 red peppers, sliced
- ½ cup walnuts, chopped

DRESSING

- 1 small lemon
- ¼ cup fresh lemon juice
- ½ cup olive oil
- 1 tsp. honey
- 1 ½ tsps. garlic, minced
- 1 tsp. salt
- ½ tsp. black pepper
- 1 tbsp. fresh thyme, chopped (or 1 tsp. dried thyme)

INSTRUCTIONS

1 To make the **Whole Lemon Dressing**, very thinly slice lemon (don't peel it); discard seeds. Finely chop the slices and put into a small mason jar. Add lemon juice, olive oil, honey, garlic, salt, black pepper, and thyme. Shake well.

2 Cook brown rice according to package directions to make 4 servings.

3 Toast sesame seeds in a dry skillet over medium heat 6 to 8 minutes, shaking skillet often.

4 Shred cabbage and slice sugar snap peas; toss into a big bowl and stir in ¼ cup of the Whole Lemon Dressing. Stir in the sesame seeds and cilantro.

5 Using a vegetable peeler, shave carrots into ribbons.

6 Divide the rice, black beans, and cabbage mixture among serving bowls. Add carrots, sliced red pepper, and walnuts.

7 Serve with the remaining dressing.

Using the whole lemon may seem a little unconventional, but it works. The resulting dressing will be a little tangy and slightly bitter.

Crispy Tofu & Rice

SERVES 4 **VEGETARIAN**

INGREDIENTS

1 pkg. white rice (enough for 4 servings)

1 tsp. ground cumin

½ lime juice

14-ounce block extra-firm tofu

Salt, to taste

¼ cup hot vegetable oil

2 garlic cloves, minced

2 tsps. ground coriander

1 tsp. smoked paprika

1 tsp. ground cumin

½ tsp. ground fennel

1 tbsp. chili sauce

2 tsps. hot sauce

1 cup water

1 cup red cabbage

1 cup fennel

2 avocados

Garnish: Feta cheese, lime slices

INSTRUCTIONS

1 Prepare rice according to package directions to make 4 servings; stir in ground cumin lime juice. Divide among serving bowls.

2 Squeeze excess water from tofu; tear into 1" pieces and season with salt. Cook in vegetable oil over medium-high heat until light brown. Cut tofu pieces in half with a spatula; cook until crisp on all sides. Reduce heat to medium. Add garlic, coriander, paprika, ground cumin, and fennel. Cook until deep golden brown. Stir in chili sauce. Add hot sauce and water; simmer until sauce thickens slightly.

3 Chop red cabbage and fennel and peel and slice 2 avocados; add to bowls. Top with feta, prepared tofu, and lime slices.

4 Serve with pan sauce from tofu.

Vegan Burrito Bowls

SERVES 2   **VEGAN**

INGREDIENTS

- 1 pkg. brown rice (enough for 2 servings)
- 15-ounce can pinto beans
- 2 chipotle peppers, chopped
- ½ lime juice
- Sea salt and black pepper, to taste
- 1 red bell pepper, sliced
- 1 green bell pepper, sliced
- 1 tsp. olive oil
- 2 Portobello mushroom caps
- Adobo sauce, to taste
- ½ cup guacamole
- ½ cup salsa
- Garnish: Arugula, lime wedges

INSTRUCTIONS

1 Cook brown rice according to package directions to make 2 servings.

2 Drain and rinse pinto beans and dump into a bowl. Add chipotle peppers, a little olive oil, lime juice, sea salt, and black pepper; stir to combine.

3 Char bell peppers in olive oil; season with sea salt and black pepper. Remove from skillet. Coat Portobello mushroom caps with olive oil and adobo sauce; season with salt and pepper. Char and slice.

4 Divide arugula, beans, rice, mushrooms, and peppers into serving bowls. Serve with lime wedges, guacamole, and salsa.

Jerk Chicken & Rice
with Pineapple Sauce

SERVES 4

MEAL

- 1 pkg. basmati rice (enough for 4 servings)
- 15-ounce can red beans
- 2 tbsps. fresh cilantro, chopped
- 2 tsps. paprika
- 1 tsp. garlic powder
- Salt, to taste
- ¼ cup Jamaican jerk seasoning
- 8 boneless chicken thighs
- 1 tbsp. canola oil
- 1 large red bell pepper, diced
- Sweet Fried Plantains (see page 124)
- 2 avocados
- 1 tbsp. lime juice
- 2 mangos

SAUCE

- 1 cup fresh pineapple, diced
- ¼ cup honey
- 1 tbsp. ketchup
- 2 tsps. Dijon mustard
- 2 tsps. lime juice
- 2 chipotle peppers in adobo, chopped
- 1 to 2 tsps. adobo sauce
- 1 tsp. garlic powder
- 2 tsps. sugar
- Salt and black pepper, to taste

INSTRUCTIONS

1 Cook basmati rice according to package directions to make 4 servings.

2 Drain and rinse red beans and warm in the microwave. Stir in cilantro, paprika, garlic powder, and salt; stir into the cooked rice. Keep warm.

3 Using Jamaican jerk seasoning, season both sides of chicken thighs. Heat canola oil in a big skillet over medium heat and cook chicken until done (165°F), turning to brown both sides. During the last couple of minutes, add red bell pepper, cooking until crisp-tender. Slice the chicken. Keep warm.

4 To make the **Pineapple Sauce**, put the pineapple and any accumulated juice into a small saucepan over medium-low heat; add honey, ketchup, mustard, lime juice, chipotle peppers plus adobo sauce, garlic powder, and sugar. Simmer for 5 to 10 minutes; season with salt and black pepper.

5 Make **Sweet Fried Plantains**.

6 Peel and slice avocados; mash and stir in lime juice. Peel and slice mangos.

7 Put rice and beans in serving bowls. Add chicken, bell pepper, mangos, and avocados. Serve with sauce and plantains.

Sweet Fried Plantains

VEGAN   **SNACK**

INGREDIENTS

2 large ripe plantains*

2 tbsps. canola oil

Coarse sea salt,
  to taste

INSTRUCTIONS

1 Cut the ends from plantains. Peel and cut into crosswise diagonal slices, ¼" to ½" thick.

2 Heat canola oil in a medium skillet (not nonstick) over medium-low heat until shimmering. In batches, add the plantains in a single layer and fry until brown on the bottom. Flip the pieces and fry until brown on the second side.

3 Transfer plantain pieces from the skillet to paper towels or a heatproof cooking rack set over a pan and sprinkle immediately with coarse sea salt. Serve warm.

Similar to bananas in appearance, but plantains are eaten cooked. For this recipe, choose plantains that are yellow-brown with black spots. The riper the plantains, the sweeter they will be when cooked.

Ginger & Garlic Peanuts

SNACK

INGREDIENTS

1 lb. shelled raw peanuts

2 tbsps. peanut oil

2 tbsps. soy sauce

6 garlic cloves, minced

1 tbsp. fresh ginger, grated

1½ tsps. fish sauce

1½ tsps. sugar

Coarse salt and black pepper, to taste

INSTRUCTIONS

1 Preheat oven to 325°F. Dump peanuts evenly onto a rimmed baking pan. Bake until just beginning to brown, 10 to 15 minutes.

2 While peanuts are cooking, in a medium bowl, whisk together the peanut oil, soy sauce, garlic, ginger, fish sauce, and sugar.

3 Remove peanuts from the oven and stir them into the soy sauce mixture until evenly coated. Return the coated nuts to the baking pan and bake an additional 10 to 15 minutes, until light golden brown.

4 Remove from the oven and immediately sprinkle with coarse salt and black pepper to taste.

Mango, Black Beans & Rice
with Tahini-Lime Dressing

SERVES 2 VEGAN

MEAL

Ginger & Garlic Peanuts (see page 125)

1 pkg. white rice (enough for
 2 servings)

1½ cups sugar snap peas

1 cup black beans, drained & rinsed

1 cup cabbage, shredded

1 carrot, sliced

1 cucumber, sliced

1 mango, sliced

DRESSING

2 tbsps. tahini

2 tbsps. rice vinegar

2 tbsps. lime juice

2 garlic cloves, minced

2 tsps. sugar

½ tsp. Sriracha sauce

INSTRUCTIONS

1 Make **Ginger & Garlic Peanuts**.

2 Make **Tahini-Lime Dressing*** by whisking together ingredients.

3 Cook rice according to package directions to make 2 servings.

4 Blanche sugar snap peas in boiling water for a minute or two then plunge into ice water; drain.

5 Divide rice, snap peas, and black beans among serving bowls. Add a little cabbage, carrot, cucumber, and mango to each.

6 Top with prepared peanuts and serve with dressing.

*Make Tamari-Lime Vinaigrette instead by using tamari in place of the tahini called for in the Tahini-Lime Dressing above.

Black-Eyed Peas, Eggs & Rice
with Tangerine Dressing

SERVES 2 VEGETARIAN

MEAL

- 1 pkg. white rice (enough for 2 servings)
- 1 tbsp. olive oil
- ½ cup yellow onion, diced
- ½ cup celery, diced
- 1 garlic clove, minced
- ½ cup red bell pepper, diced
- ½ jalapeño, finely chopped
- 2 cups baby spinach
- 14-ounce can black-eyed peas, drained & rinsed
- 2 eggs
- Sea salt, to taste
- Ground white pepper, to taste
- Paprika, to taste

DRESSING

- 1 tangerine
- ½ tsp. ground ginger
- 1 tbsp. olive oil
- 2 tsps. white wine vinegar
- 1 tsp. Sriracha sauce
- 1 tbsp. Greek yogurt
- ¼ tsp. sea salt,
- ¼ tsp. ground white pepper
- 1 tbsp. roasted pepita seeds

You can make the dressing using an orange instead of a tangerine if you prefer. What's the difference? A tangerine is less acidic and sweeter than an orange.

INSTRUCTIONS

1 To make **Tangerine Dressing**, zest tangerine; set aside. Peel and segment the fruit and add segments to a food processor. Add ginger, olive oil, white wine vinegar, Sriracha sauce, Greek yogurt, sea salt, ground white pepper, and roasted pepita seeds. Process until smooth. Stir in set-aside zest. Refrigerate until needed.

2 Cook rice according to package directions to make 2 servings.

3 Heat olive oil in a big skillet. Add the onion and celery; sauté until just beginning to soften. Add the garlic and cook for 1 minute. Add bell pepper and jalapeño and cook until crisp-tender. Add spinach, stirring until wilted.

4 Warm black-eyed peas in the microwave.

5 Divide rice, black-eyed peas, and the veggie mixture among serving bowls.

6 Cook eggs sunny-side-up or to desired doneness; season with sea salt, ground white pepper, and paprika. Add to bowls. Serve with dressing.

Spinach, Squash & Brown Rice

SERVES 4 **VEGETARIAN**

INGREDIENTS

1 butternut squash

6 tbsps. olive oil

Salt and black pepper, to taste

1 pkg. brown rice (enough for 4 servings)

1 lemon

1 tsp. Dijon mustard

1 tbsp. honey

2 cups baby spinach

1 cup Castelvetrano olives, halved

Garnishes: Grated Pecorino Romano cheese, chopped walnuts

INSTRUCTIONS

1. Preheat the oven to 400°F. Peel butternut squash, discard the seeds, and cut squash into ½" cubes. Dump onto a rimmed baking pan and drizzle with 2 tbsps. olive oil, tossing to coat all the pieces. Season with salt and black pepper and bake until tender and lightly browned, about 25 minutes.

2. While squash is cooking, cook brown rice according to package directions to make 4 servings.

3. Zest and juice lemon; set zest aside and pour the juice into a small bowl. Whisk in mustard and honey; slowly whisk in ¼ cup olive oil and season with salt and black pepper.

4. In a big bowl, stir together the rice, 2 cups of the squash cubes (refrigerate the rest for another recipe), spinach, olives, and the mustard mixture; divide among serving bowls.

5. Top each bowl with some Pecorino Romano cheese, walnuts, and the set-aside lemon zest.

Sweet & Sour Beef on Rice

SERVES 4

INGREDIENTS

6.2-ounce pkg. long grain
& wild rice with herbs
& seasonings
1 lb. ground beef
¼ cup soy sauce
⅓ cup sweet & sour sauce
1 tbsp. curry paste
2 red bell peppers, sliced
1 red onion, sliced
1 tbsp. butter, melted
1 tbsp. canola oil
Garnishes: Cilantro,
sesame seeds

INSTRUCTIONS

1 Cook long grain & wild rice according to package directions.

2 Meanwhile, cook ground beef until no longer pink,
crumbling it as it cooks; drain. Stir in soy sauce, sweet & sour
sauce, and curry paste.

3 Sauté red bell peppers and red onion in a combination of
butter and canola oil until tender.

4 Divide rice, ground beef, and vegetables among
serving bowls.

5 Top with cilantro and sesame seeds. Serve with additional
sweet & sour sauce.

Buffalo Chicken & Cauli Rice

SERVES 3

INGREDIENTS

10-ounce pkg. frozen
riced cauliflower

¾ lb. rotisserie chicken

¼ to ½ cup buffalo sauce

12-ounce pkg. broccoli slaw

1 cup cherry tomatoes, sliced

2 scallions, sliced

1 celery stalk, chopped

1 bottle ranch dressing

INSTRUCTIONS

1 Heat riced cauliflower according to package directions.

2 Shred rotisserie chicken and toss with buffalo sauce.

4 Divide riced cauliflower, half broccoli slaw, and chicken among serving bowls. Add tomatoes, scallions, and celery.

5 Serve with ranch dressing and additional buffalo sauce.

Turkey, Roasted Veggies & Rice
with Special Sauce

SERVES 4

MEAL

1 pkg. white rice (enough for 4 servings)

1½ tsps. salt

1½ tsps. black pepper

1 tsp. garlic powder

1 lb. cauliflower

1 lb. brussels sprouts

3 tbsps. olive oil

1 cup cherry tomatoes

1 lb. ground turkey

½ tsp. chipotle powder or chili powder

SAUCE

½ cup mayonnaise

1 tbsp. ketchup

1 tsp. lemon juice

½ tsp. hot sauce

½ tsp. paprika

½ tsp. garlic powder

½ tsp. ground mustard

½ tsp. salt

INSTRUCTIONS

1 Cook white rice according to package directions to make 4 servings. Fluff with a fork and stir in ½ tsp. each salt, black pepper, and garlic powder.

2 Preheat oven to 425°F. Cut cauliflower into flat florets and dump onto a rimmed baking pan. Trim and halve sprouts and add to the pan. Drizzle with olive oil and mix to coat the veggies. Arrange in a single layer and sprinkle with ½ tsp. each salt, black pepper, and garlic powder. Bake for 20 to 30 minutes, until crisp-tender. After 10 minutes, add cherry tomatoes to the baking pan; drizzle with olive oil and sprinkle with salt and black pepper. Finish baking.

3 Meanwhile, cook ground turkey in a skillet over medium heat until no longer pink, crumbling it while it cooks; drain. Stir in ½ tsp. each salt, black pepper, and chipotle powder.

4 Make the **Special Sauce** by stirring together ingredients.

5 Divide the rice among serving bowls. Add the ground turkey and veggies. Serve with sauce.

Like every recipe in this book, this one is easy to customize. Swap out cauliflower and Brussels sprouts with sweet potatoes and asparagus, or replace ground turkey with pork or beef. The Special Sauce makes a great dip or sandwich spread, too.

Brat Coins & Cauliflower Rice
with Cheese Sauce

SERVES 2

MEAL

- 1 head cauliflower
- 1 tbsp. olive oil
- 2 brats
- 6 oz. baby bella mushrooms
- 3 leeks

SAUCE

- 8-ounce block sharp cheddar cheese
- ⅔ cup beer of choice (I used an IPA)
- ½ tsp. paprika
- ¼ tsp. garlic powder
- ¼ tsp. salt
- 1 tsp. Worcestershire sauce

INSTRUCTIONS

1 Chop off flourets from cauliflower head*. Toss the cauliflower flourets into a food processor and process until rice-sized pieces form.

2 To make the **Cheese Sauce**, finely shred block of cheese** into a medium saucepan. Add beer, paprika, garlic powder, salt, and Worcestershire sauce. Heat over medium-low heat, whisking until cheese is melted and the sauce is nice and smooth; keep warm.

3 In a big skillet, heat olive oil over medium-high heat. Slice brats, add to the skillet, and cook until browned; remove brats from skillet and set aside. Keep drippings in skillet.

4 Slice mushrooms and leeks; add to the drippings remaining in the skillet, adding more oil if necessary. Cook until softened. Add 2½ cups of the riced cauliflower to the mushroom mixture and cook about 5 minutes longer. Season with salt and black pepper.

5 Divide the cauliflower mixture among serving bowls and add the brat slices. Serve with sauce.

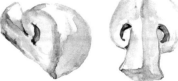

*One average-sized head of cauliflower will yield approximately 3½ to 4 cups of "rice." Store the remainder in the fridge for another use.
**Shredding the cheese yourself will provide the best results. It melts more smoothly and tastes better too!

Fajita Steak & Cauliflower Rice

SERVES 2

INGREDIENTS

3 limes

½ cup pineapple juice

5 tsps. garlic, minced

2 tbsps. honey

1 tbsp. ground cumin

1 tsp. chili powder

¼ tsp. cayenne pepper

⅓ cup cilantro

1 tsp. sea salt

1 tsp. dried oregano

½ tsp. black pepper

1 lb. flank steak

4 tbsps. canola oil

1 large red onion

1 poblano pepper

1 green bell pepper

1 red bell pepper

1 yellow bell pepper

(2) 12-ounce pkgs. frozen riced veggies (I used cauliflower with peas and carrots)

¼ cup water

½ cup cilantro, chopped

Salt and black pepper, to taste

Garnishes: Sour cream, guacamole, salsa, sliced jalapeño peppers

INSTRUCTIONS

1 In a big, zippered plastic bag, mix together the zest and juice of 1 lime, pineapple juice, 4 tsps. garlic, honey, ground cumin, chili powder, cayenne pepper, cilantro, sea salt, oregano, and black pepper; add flank steak and marinate at least 30 minutes or up to overnight. Remove the steak, pat dry, and set at room temperature for 30 minutes; discard marinade.

2 Heat 2 tbsps. canola oil in a big cast iron skillet over high heat. Add the steak and cook until desired doneness; transfer to a plate, tent with foil for 10 minutes, then slice across the grain into strips.

3 Dice onion, poblano pepper, and bell peppers. Add 1 tbsp. canola oil to the skillet, lower heat to medium, and add 1 tsp. garlic. After 30 seconds, add the onion and peppers, cooking until crisp-tender.

4 In a separate big skillet, heat 1 tbsp. canola oil. Add frozen riced veggies and water. Cook according to package directions. Remove from heat, add the zest and juice of 2 limes, cilantro, salt, and black pepper. Divide among serving bowls with steak and pepper mixture.

5 Top with sour cream, guacamole, salsa, and jalapeños.

Chicken, Citrus & Wild Rice

SERVES 2

INGREDIENTS

4-ounce pkg. wild rice

1 ½ cups chicken broth

7 tsps. olive oil

2 tbsps. rice vinegar

1 tbsp. mint, chopped

Salt and black pepper, to taste

1 chicken breast

Garlic powder, to taste

4 cups kale, chopped

1 apple, diced

1 orange, diced

½ cup goat cheese

¼ cup dried cranberries

INSTRUCTIONS

1 Cook wild rice according to package directions, using chicken broth for the cooking liquid. Remove from heat, drain, and fluff with a fork. Stir in 2 tbsps. olive oil, rice vinegar, mint, salt, and black pepper.

2 Season chicken breast with salt, black pepper, and garlic powder. Cook in 1 tsp. olive oil over medium-high heat until done; shred.

3 Mix kale, warm rice, and chicken; divide among serving bowls. Add apple and orange.

4 Top with goat cheese and cranberries.

Quick Greek Rice Bowls

SERVES 2 VEGETARIAN

INGREDIENTS

8.5-ounce pkg. heat & serve rice medley

1 tbsp. Greek vinaigrette

1 avocado, sliced

2 cups cherry tomatoes, halved

½ cup feta cheese

2 cups Greek olives, pitted

Fresh parsley, to taste

INSTRUCTIONS

1　Heat rice medley according to package directions. Divide among serving bowls.

2　Add Greek vinaigrette to each bowl; stir to combine.

3　Top bowls with avocado slices, cherry tomatoes, feta cheese, Greek olives, and parsley.

4　Serve with additional vinaigrette.

Index

Note: Recipe titles followed by an asterisk (*) indicate vegetarian recipes; two asterisks (**) indicate vegan recipes. For sauces, refer to ingredients or associated bowl recipe.